Changing
Places *To Another*
Right Place

Changing
Places
To Another Right Place

The White Feather Press

O.A. Bud Ham

First Edition
First Printing, 2006
Second Printing, 2014

COVER DESIGN: Cuinn Springer
SKETCHES BY: Retta Va Springer
BOOK DESIGN: Bob Schram
COMPACT DISC MUSIC AND AUDIO PRODUCTION:
   Aaron Baashirian and Ben Kammin

ISBN 978-0-9646397-1-3

A c k n o w l e d g m e n t s

WITH GREAT APPRECIATION to Terri McAvoy, Chris Little, Matt Dugan, Michael Ham, and a host of friends for editing suggestions given with compassion.

To Jandy Ham-Dugan for help, support and encouragement.

To Retta Va Springer and Cuinn Springer for the illustration art and book cover.

I also acknowledge the patience of many friends who have waited long for this now finished book, which I would have be a contribution to work that will never be finished.

*This book is for my wife Judy,
she is my #1 partner in life,
my best friend,
and my soul mate.*

*Relationship without freedom
Is bondage.*

*Relationship without equality
Is servitude.*

*Relationship with freedom and equality
Is a requirement of unconditional Love.*

CHANGING PLACES
To Another Right Place

"to enjoy peace in our time"

I do not like the world the way it is now.
Must I accept it?

I cannot change the world,
Or can I?

The world's greatest thinkers say we are all one.
Are they right?

If so, if I change me, I change humankind,
and the world.

Can I do that?

"To be sure," the wise man said.
I choose to change.

To my dear friends who are experiencing a more traditional spiritual journey

I HAVE BEEN A SEEKER OF SPIRITUAL TRUTH for over 57 years as this is being written. My journey has never been boring. At times it has been agonizing and even frightening. Those times are insignificant when compared to the joyous excitement, peace, prosperity and fulfillment being a spiritual seeker (spiritual risk-taker) has brought me.

May your spiritual journey—be it traditional or avant-garde—bring you the quality of life and the spiritual growth you seek.

Contents

Acknowledgments   iii

Prelude   1

Introduction   3

Chapter One
OUR UNSEEN FRIENDS   17

Chapter Two
SEEKING THE PATH TO JOY AND BECOMING   41

Chapter Three
OLD MESSAGES AND A NEW MESSENGER   63

Chapter Four
HELLO! IS ANYONE HOME?   77

Chapter Five
TURNING POINTS   87

Chapter Six
THINKING OUTSIDE THE BOX   103

Chapter Seven
SPIRITUAL GUIDANCE   117

Chapter Eight
PARTING SHOTS AT RANDOM TARGETS   147

Afteword   179

AN AUTOBIOGRAPHICAL SKETCH

FOR MORE THAN THIRTY YEARS O. A. "Bud" Ham has been president of a consulting firm he founded presently known as O. A. Bud Ham Consulting. He is a public speaker and a behavioral and relationship consultant to individuals, couples, businesses and the professions. He is also an author, an outdoorsman, and a poet. When questioned about his consulting and organization development objectives, Bud says he helps individuals and organizations know how to develop trust-based relationships and to know they have the choice of making love-based decisions rather than the more common fear-based ones. He is an unfettered advocate of practical spirituality in our personal and professional lives.

His first book, *You Are In The Right Place* is recognized as a major contribution toward helping people live with less fear in their lives. Through that work he has helped many people accept the axiom, "Life is difficult, but the solutions to our problems are not complicated." In addition to maintaining that spirituality is practical, *The Right Place* and *Changing Places*, also advance the idea and the means to test it for ourselves. Both books also advocate diversity.

As the titles of the books suggest everyone is in the right place, regardless of differences in race, life style orientation, gender, values, or beliefs.

CHANGING PLACES
To Another Right Place

THOSE WHO ARE ATTUNED to mystical/spiritual teachings believe they see the beginning signs of the "thousand years of peace" to be ushered in with the promised coming of the Golden Age, sometimes referred to as the Age of Aquarius. For we who believe this is true, such thinking is energizing and allows us to experience the great joy of positive expectations. This transformational change in human thinking, behavior, and environment has been heralded in the prophecies of mystics for thousands of years.

However, as we begin the new millennium there is great anguish and pessimism among most of humankind. With the exception of an occasional human-interest story, newspapers and news broadcasts are filled with news of the terrible things people do to one another. It seems that to be newsworthy even the weather must be devastating. On every hand we see evidence of evil in our world. Violence and death on the streets of our cities are commonplace. Death from terrorism is now a global concern. People are starving and being killed around the globe because of "holy wars," the ultimate oxymoron.

Nothing can be more unholy than for some of God's children to kill others because they follow a different spiritual master.

At this time we can only imagine what could happen when a critical number of the human population begin to think there is at least a possibility of a world at peace. This book is dedicated to making a contribution to that line of thinking. Although belief in the Golden Age has not yet influenced most people there is, in fact, a proliferation and widespread distribution of information supportive of such a change in thought. There are increasing numbers of books and other written materials on spiritual self-help which espouse that there is only one God; the God of love, only one religion; the religion of love, and only one doctrine; the doctrine of joy through forgiveness. There is evidence to suggest that many people in all major religions fear *inclusivity*, yet the availability and acceptance of the positive information, *"We are all one"* is at an all time high.

Many of the books on the bestseller lists clearly appeal to humankind's nobler emotions and are tolerant of differing paths of religious belief. This trend toward a higher level of inclusiveness is a fairly recent phenomenon. As long as this information is in demand by the public there is reason to hope for a change in thinking which, when it happens, will inevitably lead to a kinder and gentler world. More and more people accept the belief that God continues, even today, to offer his children enlightenment in a variety of ways. Many people frequently view these fearfully as "New Age" and evil. Let us not forget there was a time when every religion was considered "new age" by the established religions being practiced at the time of the emergence of the new thinking. There are thousands of religious paths that can lead to spiritual peace and enlightenment. If one path would suffice for all humankind there would be only one path. Let us accept that accommodating many cultures requires many religions.

❖ ❖ ❖

Crime and violence that are at an all time high are often the results of seeking happiness from material possessions. Society may have to "hit bottom" before it hurts enough to mend its ways. We should hope that the reality of the ugliness of what people are doing to each other should one day cause us to stop seeking peace, happiness, and satisfaction in non-spiritual ways. Selfishness either material as with possessions, or emotional as with jealousy in relationships, is the result of fear-based thinking and leads to defensiveness that can spawn violence. It has been said, "Everytime one person feels defensive another person feels attacked." Perhaps when we realize selfishness of any kind can bring us neither peace nor happiness we will look elsewhere.

❖ ❖ ❖

One of the major problems of our time is that we are losing thousands of young people to lives of destitution, debauchery, and crime because of very profitable illegal drugs. It is troubling that most people refuse to accept a natural and spiritual law, which states, *If what you are doing is not solving the problem, it is insane to expect that more of the same effort will change the outcome.*

Those of us reared in Western societies never question so called "acts of God"—earthquakes, hurricanes, tornadoes, volcanic eruptions, devastating tides, floods, and lightning caused wild fires. Such calamities wreak untold pain and anguish on humankind.

Yet, do we question whether our attitudes and behavior have no influence on such events? Is it possible that the power of the Theory of Relativity and the power of combined thought are factors? (Quantum physicists clearly tell us that thoughts are energy.) Is it, as many of our Eastern brethren believe, that we bring these disasters upon ourselves because of the accumulated negative power of countless mean-spirited thoughts and by our denial of the laws of love?

It may be well for us to remember that Hindus and the people of other eastern religions believed in and worshiped a monotheistic God of love for many, many years before the Judeo/Christian era began. It is very likely there is much we with Mid-Eastern and Western thinking can learn from them, if we are willing to take off our spiritual blinders. Thoughts are indeed things, as the seers of old and modern quantum physicists tell us. The human mind, if allowed unfettered spirituality, is capable of creating anything.

As I am past seventy years of age it is reasonable for me to expect that I am in the final one-third of my life. It is my contention, fostered by observation that, the world is in the initial phase of undergoing a spiritual revolution. If what I believe is happening is indeed true, we may even now be entering into the Golden Age. If so those of my generation and I may live to see escalating peace and declining violence in the streets and between nations. One of the goals of this book is to contribute to that process.

Friends, we live in a world of abundance. If we are willing to put forth the thought energy and the physical energy to co-create with God and accept this age of peace, which, it is said will last one thousand years, we shall also experience worldwide prosperity. The utter waste of resources, burned up in producing machines of war, and the devastation they create, could easily feed, clothe, and house the destitute of the world. There is enough—of everything!

✧ Is this a utopian position?
✧ Indeed it is.
✧ Do I believe it is possible?
✧ Indeed I do!
✧ Do I hold any hope that this will ever happen?
✧ Yes. But that depends on me . . . and on you!

It has long been known that the basic causes of humanity's problems are not political. They are philosophical. If we humans solve our philosophical problems we will no longer be forced into repeated conflicts of a political nature. Indeed, one of the definitions of utopia is, *an ideally perfect place especially in its sociopolitical aspects.*

Do you believe you can have peace in your personal life and that I can have peace in mine? You might hesitantly say, "Yes, I suppose it is possible. But what do we have to do to have it?" I answer, "Are you willing to ask, on a continuous basis, "How can I help?" Rather than, "What's in it for me?"

If we as individuals are to share in this most desirable way of living it is imperative that we accept that spiritual laws are irrefutable. It is more than prudent,

it is pure genius to use them as managing principles in governing our personal and professional lives. I challenge you to thoroughly consider the spiritual law, *Whatever you want, give it away.*
What do you suppose is the return when one gives meanness, selfishness, jealousy, hatred, dishonesty, and pain to others? The law is irrefutable. Acceptance of this one basic law allows us, a "great knowing:" *We are in charge of our own destiny.*

I cannot know all that you must do to have peace in your life, nor do I know all that I need to do to have peace in mine. But I can suggest a very good starting place. It is the same starting place for every individual and every organized society in the world— **stop doing what isn't working!** We must abandon the insane idea that we can experience a different outcome without changing the input!

Another purpose for the content of this book is that it be used as a supplemental guide for people who are not satisfied with their personal life styles and who are willing to examine their responsibility for that life style. As Mother Theresa's song says, "Let there be peace on earth and let it begin with me."
This book is written both for people who are looking for peace in their personal lives and who are also willing to give thought and effort to help move the world toward global peace. I can assure you that the messages in it will identify and clarify some of the changes which are achievable and which would make a positive difference in our world. I can also assure you that while you read this book, and if you choose to support those messages that make sense to you, courage and an open mind will be great assets. However just by thinking, if you think about the laws

of love, you will be making a personal contribution to peace. We must never forget that all learning and change begins with thought, and those thoughts have energy!

An example of a subject requiring careful thought is capital punishment. It takes an open mind for anyone who has been in favor of the death penalty to listen with understanding, and then carefully weigh arguments about the efficacy of such punishment. This is a highly charged emotional issue. Very few thinking people are ambivalent about it. Society can only benefit from openly discussing and honestly examining such an emotionally charged and divisive issue.

✧ ✧ ✧

I am not confused regarding the controversial nature of many of the subjects contained in this writing. I cannot guarantee any reader that the perspectives advanced in this book are in accord with the Will of God. I can assure you the book has been written with an earnest and honest appeal for God's guidance that it might inspire you. I prefer the American Indian position of the three truths as noted by Ed McGaa, Eagle Man: "You might be right." "I might be wrong." "I don't know."

It is my hope that at least some of the messages contained herein, whether in the text, philosophy, stories or poetry, will have validity and lasting usefulness for every reader, and thus help each individual contribute to peace in our time. I still wholly subscribe to the philosophical position that states:

You are in the right place.

CHANGING PLACES
To Another Right Place

What is this book for? What are its purposes?

✧ To re-awaken the possibility in our thinking of the existence of mystical, super-natural Guides and Guardian Angels.

✧ To encourage and provide a means for readers to accomplish values based living and increase tolerance for disagreement, the antithesis of judgment.

✧ To encourage removal of spiritual blinders to expand our awareness.

✧ To enhance the acceptance of the personal power to make positive changes in our lives that is inherent in every human being.

✧ To advance thinking that can lead us to a one-to-one relationship with God that is founded on love and completely without fear.

✧ To demonstrate there are many paths to spiritual enlightenment and that everyone who seeks peace for self and others through love-based oneness with God will find it.

✧ To elevate the consciousness of as many people as possible, as early in their lives as possible, to accept that God is their best friend. And, as with all best friends, our wish is his command as long as it brings no harm to others or us.

✧ To further advance the concepts:
  • We are all one.
  • There is enough of everything.
  • There is nothing we must do to have God's love—it is ours unconditionally—no matter what we do.

✧ To encourage readers to explore and develop their personal ability to dialogue with God.

However, if you choose to continue to grow you can benefit immeasurably by frequently asking the following question: Is the "place" I am in now the best place in which I can grow into the spirit/person I want to become? If not, changing places may be called for. This book may provide you with direction to relocate to another right place.

The "wake up call" of the terrorist attack on the World Trade Center on September 11, 2001 clearly calls for an examination of our beliefs. It is these beliefs that must change for God's children to stop killing each other in His name. All people, of all religious persuasions must give up the ideas of "specialness," "better," and/or "We have the only true religion."

If this book helps one person give up the beliefs of exclusivity and adopt instead the position that God loves each of us unconditionally, is our best friend and **we are all one,** it will have fulfilled its purposes.

An Overview of the Current
Spiritual Beliefs of the Author

NOTE: My life's journey and history of religious/spiritual beliefs through 1993 is available in the book *You Are In the Right Place* (available from my publisher, The White Feather Press and at my web site www.budham.com).

I willingly share the following intensely personal information with any reader who is interested. It could be useful to help you understand the content of this book.

I have no need to challenge the beliefs of others or to defend my own. Any review of my spiritual beliefs must be dated because I am committed to being a continuous student. My current beliefs include but are not limited to the following:

✧ Forgiveness of others and ourselves' is the way to personal peace.

✧ Fear is an unnecessary emotion that with God's help we can eliminate from our lives.

✧ The countless turning points in our lives were not just "OK" they were perfect.

✧ In the past few years I have read Neale Donald Walsch's books *Conversations with God, books 1, 2, and 3; Friendship with God; Communion with God* and *New Revelations.* Each time I read these books or listen to them on tape I experience a higher level of peace and well being.

✧ In studying Deepak Chopra's book *How to Know God* I have identified:
  • Where I think I am in knowing God. It is satisfying and inspiring.

- Every good and loving work I do, I co-create with God.
- Our lives change in direct proportion to our love-based decision making.

✧ I have read *The Autobiography of a Yogi* by Paramahansa Yogananda. I loved the emphasis on inclusion of all spiritual paths and the Hindu philosophy of non-violence. It has increased my interest in Eastern philosophy. I am impressed with the credence Buddhists and Hindu holy men and women give to Jesus and his teaching. I believe it is to the disadvantage of Christians and people of other faiths who do not reciprocate.

✧ Several of my spiritual brothers have been attending retreats and experiencing Siddha Yoga. A part of the teaching of most Eastern spiritual philosophies is the importance of a personal teacher or "guru." I welcome any information, from any love-based source, that can contribute to my spiritual growth.

✧ After several years of intense but intermittent study of *A Course in Miracles* I have concluded that it is, at this time, my primary path of spiritual study.

✧ A thorough understanding of Jesus' teaching, *"Cast your bread on the waters and it will be returned to you multiplied"* puts us in direct and complete control of our future. It is the Christian statement of karma, *Whatever you want, give it away.*

- If you want respect, give respect to others.
- If you want cooperation, be cooperative.
- If you want recognition, give recognition.
- If you want others to listen to you, listen to them.
- If you want more love, give more love.

- If you want more money, take all you can spare and with love in your heart and without discrimination give it to anyone who needs it more than you do.
- If you want people to deal fairly with you and to treat you by the Golden Rule adopt it as your primary guiding principle.
- The reciprocal of the above seven items is also true.

✧ It is incongruent not to do unto yourself as you would do unto others or have others do unto you.

✧ Spiritual laws are irrefutable. To use them as management principles in our personal and business lives is more than prudent—it is pure genius.

GRANDPA

The old man stood
By the creek with a smile
Remembering the days gone by,
Of another stream
With rock strewn bank,
Two boys and a dog
In his mind's eye.

As he stood there,
Alone with his thoughts,
He remembered the strike of a fish.
The joy that was then
He would not release
And he made for all children
Just one wish.

Please God,
May they know the thrill
Of alone in the wild
While they are a child
So life's cup they can fulfill.

Chapter One

OUR UNSEEN FRIENDS

THE CHERISHED BELIEF in Guardian Angels has existed in the minds of many people throughout and before recorded history. This chapter might reawaken or reinforce the possibility of the existence of mystical, super-natural Guides and Guardian Angels.

"Grandpa, please tell us a story about when you were a boy."

"We've heard the bear story a lot. Tell us a different one."

"Papa, did they have cars when you were a boy?"

The five grandchildren, all younger than ten years old, were sitting on the floor in front of the fireplace. The silver haired grandfather dearly loved his small audience.

"Yes, they did have cars when I was a boy, but they didn't look much like the cars we see today."

"Would you like to hear a fishing story or about a boy who got lost in a swamp?"

"Were you that boy, Grandpa."

It was late evening on a snowy, winter day. The cheerful fire in the stone fireplace made the room delightfully warm and cozy but no child was asleep when Grandpa finished the story.

THE SWAMP ANGEL
A story about our unseen friends.

His name was Sherman William Alexander. Sherman was an old family name. He was the eldest of three children. His two younger sisters had difficulty pronouncing Sherman and he became known as Bill.

In grade school he was an average student, but he really had to work at it for he was never totally in the classroom. His body might be, but his head and heart continuously cried for freedom and they were always in the out-of-doors. He was very adept at going adventuring in his mind. As a result, in the first and second grades, he frequently carried a note home to his mother that always alluded to his daydreaming.

He knew school had to be tolerated and as the years went by he learned how to cope with the system. He knew just how much time and effort were necessary to satisfy academic requirements. To Bill, school was only an interruption that kept him from being where he really wanted to spend his time.

The Trial

By the time Bill was in high school he had become a good student. Because of this his parents had long ago given up on the idea of trying to control his adventurous spirit. He had an ally in his father, who was glad his son appreciated the wilderness more than the pool hall in town, which attracted his teenage friends.

Largely because of his mother's fears he had many discussions with his mom and dad about his forays into the places where the wild things live. He cherished his time in the cottonwood forest along the river bottom, the river itself, and even the cliffs and canyons in the uninhabited foothills southwest of town were great places to go. But his most favorite place of all was the swamp.

He had arrived at a comfortable truce with his parents. They finally had agreed to tolerate his wanderings so long as he told them where he was going, and what time he promised to be back. For several months he had been diligent in honoring their agreement.

But one day, in his favorite part of the swamp, he had stayed too long. He was unconscious of the passing of daylight as he watched his animal friends. Bill spent hours watching a family of ducks, a hen mallard and nine babies. He watched with great interest as the mother frantically called her babies into shallow water. Bill even saw the wake of a large fish and he watched in total fascination, as one of the tiny black and yellow balls of fluff became a meal to a marauding northern pike. Later, he became totally engrossed in watching two muskrats building their house.

Bill never bothered to carry water or food on his outings, and it was hunger and thirst that finally got his attention. Only then did he become fully aware that the sun had set and darkness was swiftly approaching, and he suddenly remembered the time he and some of his friends had lost their way in the swamp in full daylight.

Bill hurried as fast as he could on the dim trail leading out of the swamp and headed toward the cottonwood forest where the going would be much easier. The faintly discernable trail crossed shallow waterways, and doubled back on itself as it threaded its way between deep bogs of stagnant water, black muck, and very dangerous quicksand.

There were tales aplenty about the deadly bog, such as the one about three escaped convicts who chose the swamp as part of their escape route. One was recaptured and told how his cohorts had disappeared forever in the slimy muck.

The rapidly failing light was compounding his problem. When Bill realized he had crossed only two of the three double-backs in the trail, he had to suppress the panic that threatened to explode in his gut.

He remembered a lesson from his high school biology class about night vision, and about the rods and cones in the eyes, so Bill concentrated on forcing his eyelids open as wide as he could to gather as much of the fading light as possible. A few minutes later, as the fear he had allowed himself to entertain was again growing into a full-blown panic, he knew he was close to the last double back in the trail.

With a deep breath, some of his confidence returned, and his mind raced ahead to mentally visualize the rest of the swamp trail. The remaining double back was the last really dangerous stretch of trail he would have to negotiate before emerging from the swamp and entering the forest a full mile away. Bill moved quickly. Too quickly! He stepped into what he thought was the last shallow waterway. Immediately he reacted with total panic. He had misjudged the location of the last double-back in the trail.

Instantly Bill was up to his buttocks in the black muck and stinking swamp water that covered it. His panic-stricken reaction of pumping his legs caused him to sink deeper and the slime was quickly over his belt.

The many stories he had heard about such death traps caused him to know that continuing to struggle in a panic would cause him to sink deeper and deeper into the bog. He realized that if that happened he would die and his body would never be found. This awareness created a profound state of alertness. He now knew that even the slightest unnecessary movement added to the danger.

Bill remained motionless, except for shallow breathing, and still he could feel himself sinking very slowly. In the forced stillness he soon felt an unaccustomed calmness, and strangely felt very secure. He wondered if this is how a person feels just before death. In the darkness he remembered a few lines from a poem his grandfather had written before Bill was born:

There is One who knows our every plight.
He is on the trail with us both day and night.
His promise to us is very clear.
"Trust Me, all is well. Have no fear."

The old poem was about a cowboy talking to God when he was lost in a mountain blizzard. He was quite sure his grandfather was that cowboy. He also remembered what his grandfather taught about spirituality. In his gruff, earthy way he said, "Prayer is practical, it's not pie-in-the-sky myth."

Because of a heavy blanket of clouds overhead the darkness was almost total. In this blackness he knew he could never escape from this natural grave without help. This was the first time in Bill's young life that he had felt utterly helpless because he knew there was no one to help him. In the quiet of his mind he went back to his grandfather's words about "prayer being practical." In Bill's desperation he decided to try it. He surprised himself by speaking out loud to God.

He continued to slowly sink in the quicksand.

Moments later he was sure God had provided him with a miracle. There was one sudden, bright flash of lightning. Only one. But it was enough. In that one second he saw a branch of a small sapling almost within his reach. With the aid of a short stick he was able to grasp the thin tree. He knew he would need a grip much closer to the base of the small sapling before beginning the slow process of gently pulling himself out without moving his feet or legs. Bill bent forward from the waist to extend his reach. He leaned slowly forward, until his chin touched the stagnant water while he slid his hand down the small trunk toward its thicker base.

STORM

I stand alone. Or so it seems.
The storm comes. And still I stand.
Can it be me. Flesh and bone, alone?
The storm departs. And I smile, proudly.
Then I see a tree, blown down.
Was it just me?
Did I stand, alone?

Bill prayed that the small tree would be strong enough as he began the agonizingly slow process of trying to overcome the suction of the quicksand while using only the muscles of his upper body. He successfully fought the temptation to use the greater strength of his legs, which would cause him to sink deeper.

He pulled with all his strength. It seemed an eternity before he experienced the first movement. Then he knew he had begun breaking the vacuum-like suction on his body, but when he periodically released his grip and rested his arms he could feel the loss of some of his hard-earned progress. Finally, he started to relax only one arm at a time to check his losses. Then with renewed strength he continued his battle with nature's vacuum.

Bill's progress buoyed his spirits. His mouth was dry and his breath began coming in great gasps, but he continued the struggle relentlessly. Then, with no warning, there was a heart-stopping snap as the small tree broke. Hope was now gone as he quickly started to lose the slight gains he had made.

As fear started to take control of him a strong feminine voice said, "Lean backward, lean back now. Then you can pull your feet out of your boots."

He immediately did as he was instructed. As soon as he did he felt the release of the pressure on his feet. Gentle steady pulling allowed him to free one foot, and then the other from his pull-on boots. Soon he was lying on his back, with both legs extended on top of the muck. Bill was nearly exhausted, but he was able to keep most of his face and his nose above the stinking water. Then the voice spoke again, "Roll to your left." A few seconds later he was pulling himself back onto firm ground. When his breathing became more normal he said in a subdued voice, "Are you still here? Who are you?"

Silence was his only answer.

Nearly exhausted with sweat pouring down his face and his arm muscles cramping, he sat cross-legged on the trail and rested. As sweat rolled down his cheeks he thanked his long dead grandfather and the unseen feminine Source.

Bill had not fully recovered his strength and equilibrium as he cautiously began picking his way through the darkness along the trail. He very quickly realized his bare feet were going to suffer terribly and he found he had missed the double back on the trail by only about twenty feet. In the darkness it was slow going but the biology lesson on eyesight helped. In that lesson he had also learned it was helpful to focus your eyes to the side of what you want to see rather than looking directly at it. He also used a long stick as blind people use a cane.

As he approached the end of the swamp trail most of Bill's strength had returned. Then his heart started pounding again because he dreaded the last fifty yards of the trail where the swamp transitioned into the drier upland of the cottonwood forest. That section was overgrown by tall weeds. He had long known that if he was going to encounter a rattlesnake anywhere this was the place. He now felt especially vulnerable because of his bleeding, bare feet.

Just two weeks before, his buddy David, an old man named Monte and Bill had encountered a huge diamondback almost six feet long. It was lying coiled in the trail and seemed to defiantly dare them to pass. Monte repeatedly pounded the huge snake with a long club and mashed it into the soft, moist earth. The rattler finally accepted defeat and crawled away into the thick, high weeds.

Bill decided he would use the long stick to flail the weeds and thus warn any snake of his approach. He was thankful that neither the silent copperheads nor equally silent and deadly water moccasins lived in Colorado. Remembering his newly found "resource" for overcoming fear, Bill appealed to that Source again. Then as he made his way toward the high weeds in the deep darkness he was incredulous as an almost-full moon appeared from behind the dark clouds. Those clouds had also been the home of the heaven-sent lightning bolt. With this new gift of silver light, even with the dark shadows, Bill moved quickly through the weeds.

As soon as he emerged to the higher level of the cottonwood forest the light also allowed him to begin a fast jog. He knew he would be home in a bit over an hour. In spite of the pain in his cut and bleeding feet, the jogging pace turned into a loping run as he thought about the fear he knew his mother and father must have been feeling. And Bill kept thinking about how he had violated their agreement.

Bill knew that when his parents saw his bruised and bleeding feet and smelled the stench of the swamp slime with which he was covered he would have to tell them what had happened. He also knew they would forgive his indiscretion. As his pace quickly closed the distance to home, and food, and a warm kitchen, he again recalled his grandfather's words. "Prayer is practical – its not pie in the sky myth." Yes, he silently agreed, spirituality is indeed practical.

As he emerged from the cottonwood forest he knew the lights of an approaching vehicle would be from his dad's pickup truck as he searched for his overdue son.

It was a joyful reunion with his mother and sisters and the family enjoyed the delayed evening meal. Bill told them about his battle with the bog when he stepped off the trail and that explained the missing boots. He told them he was sorry for causing them concern but gave them no other details.

In the succeeding months he was even less involved in the things most teenage boys are concerned about. Bill had long been an avid reader of books about nature, and now he also wanted to know about the spiritual world. He read every book he could find about parapsychology and angels. His swamp experience led to his introduction to beliefs and concepts he had never heard about in his fundamentalist Christian environment. Strange sounding words such as "extrasensory perception," "psychic phenomena," "karma," and "reincarnation" entered Bill's vocabulary. Bill read about the life of Edgar Cayce, known as the sleeping prophet of Virginia Beach. That was followed by a short biography of Walter Russell, which introduced him to the concept of *Universal Mind*. He dearly loved struggling through the proper but antiquated writing of Ralph Waldo Emerson. After he read *The Gospel of Emerson,* the poet became his spiritual hero.

His mother noticed the change in his reading habits and she was the only one to notice that he had changed; he was quieter and more serene than before. Her gentle quizzing finally led him to tell her the whole story. After he finished she held him close as tears streamed down her face.

Bill frequently thought about the near disaster in the swamp. His taciturn personality, combined with the bizarre nature of his experience, made it impossible for him to speak of the event to any of his friends. He easily dismissed any fearful thoughts about his brush with death. Instead he savored the warm, comfortable feeling that came to him each time he remembered his new insight that now he knew he had a powerful, unseen friend. The experience changed Bill's thinking, and therefore his life. In his internal dialogue he now referred to the unseen entity of his encounter as his "Swamp Angel." Bill experienced a peaceful transition to another right place. He was never quite the same, and he never felt alone again.

Guides and Guardian Angels—More About Our Silent Friends

To my conscious knowledge, I have never seen one. Yet, I firmly believe I have been in their presence, interacted with them and conversed with them. I just didn't know they were angels. In ancient times angels were lumped together with archetypes—gods and goddesses of yesteryear. Today few would believe archetypal gods and goddesses have influenced their life. Not so with angels. No other paranormal beliefs have existed as long, or are as widespread, as belief in angels. I personally experienced the following incidents. I will leave it up to you to decide whether or not intervention with angels was involved.

Death in a Blizzard

In my life I have driven well over one million miles and, as this is being written, I have never been involved in an accident while driving. I cannot believe it is because of great skill or blind luck. Rather, I believe my guardian angel has steered me through almost unbelievably dangerous hazards, without a scratch, on several occasions. Such as the time my son, one of my sons-in-law and I were traveling on Interstate 70, in eastern Colorado during a snowstorm.

It had been snowing hard for several hours and the pavement was covered. But traffic was light on the modern divided highway and cars and trucks were moving smoothly at about fifty miles per hour. I noticed there was a large semi-truck about one hundred yards behind me as I topped a rise and the road began a gradual decent into a shallow valley.

Immediately after beginning the decent it was like I was driving in a different world. Visibility that had been at least two hundred yards dropped to less than a hundred feet and my pickup truck fishtailed slightly on the super-slick pavement. I instantly became intensely alert.

Through the swirling snow I saw a dim outline on the road ahead. When I could finally make it out I saw it was a person waving wildly for me to stop, which I knew was probably impossible. And even if I could stop, I was sure the large tractor-trailer rig behind me could not. I had to change lanes quickly to avoid the person and a pickup truck, like mine, stopped at a crazy angle. Because of the quick turn my truck went into a slide.

I grabbed instinctively to pull the shifting lever to put the truck into four-wheel-drive. My vehicle was completely out of my control as I saw the tangled mass of cars and trucks blocking the road ahead. I saw no possibility that we would not crash into them.

The next thing I knew my wildly careening pickup was sliding backward down the hill. As the rear wheels end went off the side of the pavement the front end whipped around causing the truck to swing in a large arc, which enabled us to barely miss an overturned semi-truck. What happened next was even more unbelievable, and almost impossible to describe. All I could do was hold on. My truck first spun like a top, at least two complete revolutions, and then it was like a serpent, slithering its way through the obstacle course of crashed vehicles. We came out the other side of the mass of battered and overturned vehicles without a scratch.

When I tried to move the truck further out of harm's way, the engine was running but I had no power. I couldn't understand what was wrong. Finally I noticed the drive shift lever was in neutral instead of four-wheel drive.

Two people died in the accident and several were severely injured. Was it luck that caused me to err in the shifting? I choose to believe it was not intended for us to be involved in an accident that day and my guardian angel was doing his/her/its job.

Arthritis or Potatoes

The stiffness in the knuckles and finger joints of both of my hands was beginning to become a con-

cern to me. It was so bad that when I shook hands
with anyone with a firm grip I winced with pain. I am
an inveterate reader. One day with nothing else
handy to read I picked up a copy of a small monthly
publication on nutrition. The article I read said that
many people who had arthritic symptoms found relief
if they stopped ingesting all plants of the nightshade
family. The article went on to explain that common
plants in this family are potatoes, peppers, eggplant,
tomatoes and tobacco. I did indeed have interest in
the article because of my problem, but I dismissed it
when the writer admitted there was no scientific
research to back up the claim.

I was never a fan of the magazine and I didn't
read another one until about a year later when I
again absentmindedly picked up a recent copy. It is
not my style but for a reason, which I cannot explain,
I read a letter in the "Letters to the Editor" column.
The letter I read was from a woman who profusely
thanked the editor for the article about nightshade
and arthritis. She said because of the article about the
possible connection between arthritis and nightshade
plants she stopped serving nightshade vegetables to
her husband who was a carpenter. Within a few
weeks all of his debilitating arthritic symptoms disappeared.

It was early November when I read the letter to
the editor. I had just returned from a cold and wet,
weeklong elk hunting trip. During the trip my hands
pained me severely, especially upon arising in the
morning. Potatoes had been a favorite food in my diet
for a lifetime but the pain was so great I reluctantly
decided that immediately after Thanksgiving I would
totally eliminate them from my diet. Tomatoes, peppers, and eggplant have never been among my

favorite foods so avoiding them was quite easy. I had stopped smoking cigarettes some years before, and as a youth each time I had tried smokeless tobacco it made me deathly ill. I also remembered that as a small boy my mother had stopped preparing eggplant for our family because each time I ate it I became ill. By the following February all arthritic symptoms in my hands had disappeared.

In my activities as a public speaker and consultant I have told many people about the experience of eliminating potatoes from my diet. On subsequent contacts several people have told me about similar experiences. For example, I lectured for a day to an audience of about 200 people at the annual meeting of the District Dental Society in Springfield, Illinois. I was invited back a year later to conduct a team-building workshop. As I was walking across the hotel lobby to the conference room I saw a person running toward me. Rather than an attack, I was treated to a delightful hug from a happy and grateful young woman. Because of my presentation she had eliminated nightshade plants from her husband's diet the previous year. She joyfully told me how it had saved her husband's dental career.

About four years after first reading about the connection between nightshade and arthritis, a friend who knew about my experience wrote to tell me that an article in the New England Journal of Medicine identified the substance in nightshade plants causing these symptoms in many people.

I have tested my body's tolerance of potatoes several times in subsequent years. The results are the same, painful arthritic symptoms in some of the joints in my body within a few weeks after unrestricted ingestion of potatoes.

In my opinion the odds of me reading two articles, written one year apart, in a publication I had never read before, are small to say the least. I believe my guardian angel or spirit guides directed me.

Directed to an Artifact

For five years in the late 1950's my young family and I were privileged to live in the small mountain town of Salida, Colorado. The town is nestled in the upper Arkansas River Valley and for thousands of years prior to the incursion of settlers; the valley had been a home to American Indians.

A close friend introduced me to the hobby of hunting for Indian artifacts, primarily arrowheads. I remember how surprised I was when he told me it was not uncommon for him to find three or four in an afternoon of searching for them in the foothills near our town.

After just a couple of outings with him, and finding several broken but genuine stone arrow points, I became an amateur archeologist. It wasn't long until this hobby became a passion, which I pursued almost every weekend that the ground wasn't covered with snow. Much of the land in the area was either in one of several national forests or controlled by the Federal Bureau of Land Management and therefore open to arrowhead hunting.

At that time my primary duty as an employee of the Bell Telephone System was maintaining a microwave system used for the transmission of long-distance telephone circuits. One of the stations I maintained was located in the San Isabel National

Forest in the foothills near the base of Monarch Pass a few miles west of Salida. During the previous summer I had spent several hours looking for arrowheads in that area but had found nothing encouraging.

One afternoon in late April, I was driving into the station for a routine visit. As I drove up the long, winding dirt road to the station my thoughts again turned to artifact hunting. It had been a long winter and now the snow lay in scattered patches on the hillside in the spring sunshine. I was about halfway up the mile long road when, without thinking or planning to do so I stopped the truck, set the hand brake, and walked at least 25 yards up the hillside.

I was back in my truck and driving into the station before I realized what had happened. I had walked to a tiny patch of bare ground, picked up a small, white, perfectly formed quartz arrowhead and put it in my shirt pocket.

When I left the truck and entered the station I thought my mind had been playing tricks on me. I thought I was dreaming about stopping and leaving the truck on the drive in—until I put my hand into my shirt pocket and retrieved the perfect arrowhead.

A Supernatural Phenomenon

The setting was a campsite in the White River National Forest on Cross Creek, about twenty miles south of Vail, Colorado, and at least six miles from the nearest road. The event that had brought us into this beautiful place was a Family Backpack Seminar. My family and I served as hosts and organizers of a group of about twenty people who were all client/friends. We backpacked into the wilderness area on a Monday in late July and out on the following Friday.

Cheryl, the best friend of our eighteen-year-old daughter Jandy, had to cancel her plans to be with us because her mother, who had been ill for about a year with a brain tumor, took a sudden turn for the worse. Cheryl was like another daughter and had spent time with us many summers since her family had moved several years earlier.

About 2:00 AM on Wednesday morning Jandy came to the tent I occupied with my wife and five-year-old son. She was sobbing hysterically. After comforting her she told us that Cheryl's mother had appeared in her tent asking Jandy to have our family care for Cheryl because she no longer would be able to do so.

When we arrived home late Friday evening there was a message waiting. Cheryl's mother had died

Wednesday night. Shortly thereafter, Cheryl became our fifth daughter.

Intuitive Intervention

Beginning in 1981 and continuing through 1996 I was one of the founders and a principal in The Bob Barkely Foundation. At the time of his death in 1977, Dr. Barkley was one of the world's best known dentists and recognized as the father of preventive dentistry. The foundation was formed to sponsor an annual gathering of dentists and their families to extend Dr. Barkley's philosophy of learning and spiritual growth. We named the meeting The Rocky Mountain Rendezvous. The mission of the gathering was to improve family communications, dental team communications, and explore ways to better serve dental patients.

In the mid 1980's the Rocky Mountain Rendezvous was attended by a gay, male dentist from California. This dentist was well known in his home state for conducting team building seminars.

At the conclusion of his second visit to the Rendezvous he approached me and proposed that he be one of the presenters at the next RMR. In my assessment of our interaction I believe I was kind to him. But my fear-based prejudices of that time made it impossible for me to welcome a homosexual as a presenter.

A few months later UPS delivered a box containing three beautiful hardbound books to my home—*A Course in Miracles*—they were a gift from the above mentioned dentist. Over the next few months I made several attempts to read the two larger books; *The Text,* and the *Workbook for Students*. But they seemed much too religious—to "Christy" for me.

A short time later I received feedback from a small group of trusted friends that I had been painfully judgmental to one of our group members. I had received that feedback about my behavior many times over a span of more than 20 years. But this time I could no longer rationalize my way out of it. I committed to myself, at a very deep level, to change and become more tolerant.

I was earnestly seeking information or a "path" to help me effect the change to become less judgmental. One afternoon as I was riding my Schwinn exercise bike, on which there was a reading stand, I took one more stab at *A Course in Miracles*. This time I selected the smallest of the three books, *The Manual for Teachers*. By the time I had read the first few pages I knew that this small book contained information that could help me with my commitment to become less judgmental. I have been a student of *The Course* ever since.

A few years later, as I was lecturing at the California State Dental Convention, I visited briefly with the dentist who had sent me the Course. I told him with great sincerity of my gratitude and the value of his gift to me.

He said, "Bud, it was one of the strangest happenings in my life. I was in a bookstore and saw the three volumes. There was a powerful intuitive message that told me I must buy the books and send them to you. I have never read *A Course in Miracles,* nor do I know any one, except you, who has read it."

I shall be forever grateful for that intervention—it changed my life.

LIVING FREE

A question often comes to me,
Why do men try their souls?
They struggle hard and try to prove
The hollow victory of fools.

To add it all—our stress and pain,
We price out the bottom line.
What is it worth in gold or grain,
When measured in "future time?"

What is the purpose, our being here?
Just one grand accident?
If that is so I want it back,
The love that I have lent.

Somehow to me it doesn't seem
That any thing is free.
And if that is so the gambler's chance
To really win can never be

The books must be balanced,
Or there is no God, on this I do agree.
So as straight as I can I'll play life's game,
But right or wrong I will live free.

Chapter Two

SEEKING THE PATH TO JOY AND BECOMING

The natural quest for healthy human beings is to seek the highest quality of life for themselves and for their loved ones. *The quality of our lives is directly related to the quality of our relationships.* The goal of this chapter is to provide a means to increase values-based living and to increase tolerance for disagreement. Both are vital to strong, love-based relationships.

The Futility of Struggle

If I am struggling to become as much as I can,
I am creating the resistance to my own growth.
When I struggle I force my will on my becoming.
To become what God would have me become
requires only release, not struggle.

MORE AND MORE "AVERAGE" HUMAN BEINGS who are serious spiritual students are accepting that we are all one. I consider this line of thinking the spiritual component of Albert Einstein's law of relativity (it is no longer a theory, it's been proven), which tells us everything in the universe is connected. It therefore might be concluded that if the peace of one human is

violated, the quality of life is reduced for all
humankind.

It would be so very helpful if we all accepted three
simple sentences:

Anything I do or say that helps anyone else helps me.

Anything I do or say that hurts anyone else hurts me.

I cannot gain from another's loss nor lose from another's gain.

In my consulting business I am frequently called
upon to conduct team-building retreats. The first
major objective in my approach to team building is to
introduce participants to a relationship-building model
with a primary focus of bonding and creating trust.
Through lecture, and participative use of the model,
team members come to realize that levels of trust are
greatly influenced by the willingness to disclose various aspects of our histories and our beliefs.

Participants are invited to present their autobiographies, which can take a number of hours to complete for even a small group of eight to ten people.

Participation is encouraged, but each person has
the freedom to choose not to participate. Each is also
encouraged to seek her or his own comfort level in
disclosing life events. Only rarely does someone
choose not to participate, even though many are
somewhat uncomfortable with this intimate level of
sharing their histories. Comments made by various
participants indicate that they may think, "No one is
interested in a 'garden-variety' life such as mine." Or

perhaps the other extreme, they hesitate to share that their family was dysfunctional.

Seldom is anyone bored in these sessions. Participants find that there is no such thing as a garden variety life and are often relieved to learn that John Bradshaw, long regarded as a leading family therapist, teaches that the great majority of families are dysfunctional.

I am no longer shocked at the stories told during these sessions, but I am frequently drawn to tears. So are some of the more macho participants who almost never cry in the presence of others. The process is physically, mentally and emotionally draining, but it is an activity that is spiritually enhancing, and the healing that typically occurs is extraordinary.

Psychologist George Casper Homans demonstrated many years ago that the glue that bonds relationships is information about each other—the more personal the information, the stronger the bond. He also taught us:

"The more we know about another person the greater is the likelihood we will care for that person and they will care for us if personal information is mutually shared."

The only exception to this truth is that if this sharing identifies incompatible values we are quite likely to grow apart. It is another truism of human nature that we like to be with people with whom we share values and who see the world much the way we do. A frequent comment I make to clients and audiences is: "In any group the synergy that results from true teamwork cannot exist without the proper mix of respect and affection in that group." Frequently the response to this statement is a strong negative reaction to the word affection. A typical comment might be, "Yes, I know respect is important but what does affection have to do with getting the job done?"

My response is, "Assume you have a group of five to ten employees who must function as a team to accomplish their task. Further, let us assume that two or more of them do not like each other. Now let us visualize the same number of people, assigned the same task, where the proper mix of respect and affection is present. Which group will have more energy to direct to the achievement of their assignment?" The answer is obvious—disharmonious relationships waste a lot of energy.

The most effective way to accomplish desired bonding in a limited amount of time by shared personal information is through the presentation of autobiographies. This process enhances trust building, a necessary ingredient for teamwork to flourish.

Any negative judgment we make about another person's values or behavior is detrimental to the formation of trust, respect, and affection in any group. Our tolerance for disagreement with others is much stronger if we have knowledge of the trials and pain experienced by that person in his or her life.

Following are three personal stories told during these sessions. Only the names have been changed. I wrote the accompanying poem shortly after hearing the first painful story.

THE BEATEN HEART

He fought against the winds of chance and never saw the win.
He was battered as a little boy and didn't understand.
He thought, "That's just the way it is, no different anywhere."
Until a teacher, saw the scars and bruises in his hair.
Brother and Sister felt it too, and suffered through the pain.
The three were sent to different homes the day the sheriff
came.
One went east, another south, and Charley was sent west.
Together nevermore.
The three weren't beaten anymore, unless love's lack is pain.
In spite of that he managed, Charley became a kindly man.
He wouldn't harm another though anger burns inside.
His tears are gone, just burned away, Charley cannot cry.
In his pain he winces and he always wonders why.

Charlie's Bruises

Charley was thirty-one years old, married and the father of two small children. His peers and employer knew him as a loyal employee and a very hard worker. Unfortunately he was also considered to be arrogant and somewhat angry.

When Charley was five years old his father abandoned him, his mother, four-year-old brother and two-year-old sister. His destitute and poorly educated mother turned the children over to the county for foster care.

Charley came to believe beatings were the natural order of things. But one day, when Charley was in the first grade, as he handed something to his teacher she noticed bruises and scabs on his arm. On closer inspection she noticed still other telltale signs of child battering.

The sheriff was called and Charley and his siblings were removed from the abusive foster home. Shortly thereafter the children were separated and placed in different homes.

They were never together again. When Charley told his story he had not seen his sister or mother since the separation of more than twenty years earlier. He had seen his brother only once.

An emotional hush settled on the room after Charlie finished his autobiography. Several people dabbed tears from their eyes. After a respectful length of time I asked Charlie if he had forgiven his tormentors. He said, "I don't think so, at least not completely."

The awareness of the continuing pain Charlie felt because of these events softened the judgments by his teammates. They no longer consider him to be an angry and arrogant young man.

It was a perfect opening for me to explain to Charlie, and the group, that the act of forgiving is not intended to help those being forgiven—it is for helping the forgiver to heal and be whole.

Peter's Problem

Peter's problem, wetting the bed every night, began before he was five years old. He does not remember having it before his father died, between his fourth and fifth birthday.

His mother remarried when he was six. His macho stepfather had no tolerance for the little boy and his problem and was determined to break him of "that stupid bad habit." When spankings didn't work his next attempt was to wrap the boy in wet sheets every night when he went to bed. That didn't work either.

The next attempt to break Peter was for the boy to sleep naked in a bathtub with about three inches of cold water in it. After several nights, when this didn't work either, the stepfather beat the boy with a strap, moved out of the house and told Peter's mother he would come back when her baby quit wetting the bed. Peter's mother obtained a divorce.

As usually happens, Peter outgrew the problem. But he was still carrying the shame of that childhood problem as a mature, successful health professional.

Peter's soft-spoken eloquence and openness as he told his life's story touched the heart of every man in the small group of men in the fishing camp. We had come together for a combination of recreation and a growth experience. Peter's candid sharing of a painful experience contributed to our acceptance of him. His story added to the intimacy of the group and enabled the rest of us to be more candid as we shared our life experiences.

Beth's Dilemma

Beth had finally given up hope that she would ever have a husband and children. But she decided she would at least be independent. She obtained employment in a city several hundred miles away from her parents and the small town where she grew up.

In her new location she settled comfortably into the life of a twenty-five year old single woman. She started attending church and found good friends there. She and the minister also became friends. He was twenty-five years her senior and not married. In spite of the age difference they started dating, and in a bit over a year they were married.

Her life changed almost immediately from one of loneliness to a life of terror. What she had thought was affectionate attention now became insane jealousy on her husband's part. He beat her if she was a few minutes late getting home from work. He continually told her that she was stupid and ugly, and that she was very fortunate that he had the willingness to give her companionship in exchange for sexual activities. Beth found his sexual demands repugnant. When she resisted he raped her.

When she could no longer stand the abuse she fled to her parents' home. Her parents were staunchly religious people and had been quite happy when Beth had married a minister. Upon Beth's return they made it very plain to her she was not welcome under those conditions and she should return to her husband.

She moved in with friends until she could find employment in a different town. She obtained a divorce. Then her terror began anew. Her ex-husband began stalking her and leaving notes stating he was going to kill her as soon as "conditions" were right. When she asked for a restraining order, none of the officials she spoke with took her problem seriously. She fled again.

Now, years later, Beth has a good job and a husband who loves her. She believes the anonymity of her new name, plus the advancing age of her ex-husband make it unlikely he will bother her again.

Beth holds a high stress corporate office position with her employer. Prior to this seminar she was known as the "OB"—office bitch—her co-worker's perception of her softened remarkably following this retreat.

Fear-Based Teaching

Wife battering and child battering continue to be significant problems in our society. The Old Testament's image of a vengeful God is still being taught in some religious groups today. I believe a strong case can be made that this teaching contributes to domestic violence. If our view of our God is that of a sometimes loving but sometimes vengeful and fearsome father who severely punishes his children when they misbehave, or make mistakes, we have a model at the highest level for wife and child abuse.

One of my fundamentalist Christian friends loves me and is genuinely concerned about my salvation. He is concerned about me because of my curiosity and interest in religions other than Christianity and my willingness to study and learn from spiritual resources, which he labels Un-Christian and New Age. He sent me a tape of a sermon he thought might help me. In the sermon the minister told a story about a boy in his early teens and his sister who was slightly younger. Church attendance was a regular activity for their family. The children's parents had been called away for a weekend and left the two children on their farm. On Sunday morning the boy decided he would not go to church, instead he would stay home and work. His sister was furious with him and went to church by herself.

The sermon tells us that the boy hitched a mule to a plow and was in a field plowing. By late morning a thunderstorm developed and the boy was struck by lightning and killed. The message of the minister's sermon was that God punished the boy for not going to church, and in so doing God sent a message to everyone else.

If I believe my God is only loving and compassionate when I am behaving according to religious teaching, and is violent and fearsome when I sin or make mistakes, why wouldn't I have the responsibility, as head of my house, to deal with the behavior of my family in the same way? Would this be an appropriate place to ask the question, "What would Jesus do?"

Much of the guilt, doubt, and frustration of well-meaning, religious people springs from their inability

to be deeply committed to the "oughts" and "shoulds" of their religious organizations. Because of low commitment they frequently violate what they believe are their religious values and feel guilty when they do. If we are personally willing to take the risk of examining, questioning, and even testing these "rules," which we may see as values, we will find that we will *own* those values, which remain after our examination. When a value becomes mine it is much easier to discipline my thinking, which influences my behavior, and not violate the value.

If we violate a value on a continuous basis because of low commitment to that value, one of two things is likely to happen—we either reject the value or we develop some level of neurosis from the continuing guilt. If we have a strengthened commitment to the values we use as rules to govern our lives we will live with more peace and less fear. It is that state of being our creator and our spiritual masters want for us. If we are willing to spend the energy and take the risks associated with self-determination and self-correction we won't always be right, but we will always be growing rather than blindly attempting to obey some other human being's rules that someone has determined are spiritual.

There are many intelligent, well-educated adults who continue to rely on the words and experiences of others for all of their spiritual guidance. These words and events are usually thousands of years old, and have gone through countless interpretations and translations from one language to another, often rendering them grossly different from the original.

Perhaps a more accurate process for developing spiritually is to work at trusting the communication we receive from our creator any time we are willing to

listen. But that requires that we think as well. One of my mentors, who is blessed with wisdom and quiet dignity, has said that many people would rather die than think!

It seems that all of the world's religions put much greater emphasis on learning from the experiences of others rather than from our own. When our experience does not square with the words of someone else's experience we often deny our own experience. All the while we have an abiding knowledge that experience is indeed the best teacher.

Certainly we can use the experiences and the words of others to help us grow and discover who we are. Yet when we are confused we have just cause to examine that which confuses us. Because of confusion, inconsistency, and perceived hypocrisy many people in our society no longer accept the dogma and doctrine of organized religions. Unfortunately many of these people cast themselves adrift. They stop asking questions and may not be aware of the appropriateness of seeking their own truth.

For example, Jesus is the spiritual master of many of you reading this book. Jesus told us, "Ye are gods . . . God is our father . . . We are brothers and sisters." Yet, many religionists consider it blasphemous to say, "I too am God's child, therefore I am part of God." This dilemma is dealt with in greater detail later in this book.

I refuse to attempt to totally govern my life
based on events that other people experienced
thousands of years ago when
God talks to me every day.

RALPH WALDO EMMERSON
[paraphrased by the author]

As previously mentioned, one of the so-called New Age courses of study I have been involved in for many years is *A Course in Miracles*. There are three volumes in *The Course:* the *Text,* the *Workbook,* and the *Manual for Teachers*. It is difficult to identify, in a limited space, all I have gained from this study. Most certainly I can tell you that *The Course* was instrumental in beginning the process that allows me to live nearly fear free, and therefore with more love and peace in my life.

Lesson number 193 in the *Workbook* is, All Things are Lessons God Would Have Me Learn, and is quite relevant here. (Consider the three autobiographies on the previous pages.) The central theme of lesson 193 is, *Forgive and you will see this differently*.

The teaching in the lesson tells us that if we still have any old pain associated with a past event in our lives that one or both of two conditions still exist; we have not learned the lesson and/or, unforgiveness is hiding in our mind.

The usefulness of this lesson became clear to me after I had been studying *The Course* for about ten years. It was not the first time I had read the lesson by any means but it was the first time I applied it and seriously questioned my own old pain. I had been working on forgiveness for a good long while because of *The Course*. But this time it was different. It was time for me to use the lesson.

When I was thirteen years old my father had an affair with another woman. I re-experienced the pain from that affair quite often in my adult life because I used the event as an example for emphasizing the importance of forgiveness in the couples' retreats and personal and spiritual growth workshops that I frequently conduct. But this time I became acutely aware of the lesson as it pertained to my own life.

The lesson, and the timeliness, caused me to mentally review the long history of the event—long, because I did not forgive my father for 23 years. As I thought about it I was sure that I had forgiven my father, the other woman, and my mother for any contribution she might have made to the situation. Likewise, I was convinced that I had learned all I could from the event. I wondered what caused me to continue to feel pain because of this affair. The answer came to me with a sudden and welcome surprise—I had never forgiven myself! My pain was a result of not forgiving *myself* for the many times I had spurned my father's attempts at reconciliation.

I have learned that guilt is an unnecessary, fear-based emotion that avails us nothing other than getting our attention. When we do experience guilt it is a "wake-up call," telling us that it is appropriate to take further action to correct the mistake that triggered the guilt so that we may be rid of it.

It is not inappropriate to have regrets and indeed I do. If I had it to do over again I would most certainly have overcome my fear-based pride and forgiven my father and myself much sooner. That would have enabled us to enjoy our love and friendship during the twenty-three years I instead maintained unforgiveness.

Now, as a man in my seventies I believe the final chapter of the event that happened more than fifty-five years ago has been concluded. As I write this I feel no old pain, and I trust the event has been useful once again. It is often said that God works in mysterious ways. We may not always recognize it but His work is practical. Sometimes it takes a lifetime to understand. Sometimes it takes longer.

Examining Core Values

Earlier in this chapter I wrote of examining our values with the intent of clarifying their meaning to us personally and owning them or rejecting them. I believe this can be a beneficial, life-long process and it is necessary for growth. Wise teachers have taught us that when our values change we also change.

In lectures I have frequently referred to core values. After a lecture during which I had used the term, I reflected on my presentation. I asked myself what I would have said if anyone in the audience had asked me what my core values are. My first thought was, "Oh, but of course I know what they are. I could rattle off a list any time." I didn't find that answer very satisfying, so I determined to think the question through until I was sure I had clarity. It was a good exercise for me—one I would recommend to everyone.

I am not a numerologist, but somehow through the years the number five seems to be very useful when I consider spiritual matters, and I believe values clarification is indeed a spiritual matter. I had no intent of limiting my core values to five but once again that number seemed to be complete. The five values I have listed below are certainly not all inclusive. Some values are so much a part of our being they no longer require examination or conscious thought. Most certainly I am not suggesting these should be anyone else's core values.

There is another important step that can help me maximize the benefit I can realize by clarifying my values. It is this: If I am clear on what I want to become, clarifying my core values can contribute to the quality of decisions I must make to take me there.

The list of my dominant core values follows. I have arranged them in a specific order, not because one is more important than another, but because the acronym *MIRTH* helps me remember them.

✧ MORALITY

Morality matters, even in this materialistic society. Events at the highest levels of government have borne this out. Recently there was a spiritual joke making the rounds. (Yes, God does have a sense of humor!) It seems a group of priests, ministers, and rabbis got together and convinced Moses that he should renegotiate with God. He agreed and went up on the mountain. He returned after several days looking tired and haggard. He said to the assembled religious leaders, "I have good news and bad news. The good news is He reduced the number from ten to six. The bad news is adultery is still one of them."

Morality can be defined as striving to live by the highest mores of our society. A moral society assures our freedom and our prosperity. A moral person strives to govern his or her behavior in such a way that it will hurt no one and has the greatest possibility to contribute to the quality of his or her own life and the lives of others.

✧ INTEGRITY

One useful definition of integrity is, say what you will do and then do what you said you would do—said another way, "Walk your talk." People of integrity keep their commitments. When a person of integrity accepts a job that begins each workday at 8A.M. showing up on time is a commitment. Living with integrity includes keeping all of your promises, even those you made "off the cuff" with little or no thought. If you change your mind later, to maintain integrity, you must tell the person to whom you made the commitment.

✧ REVERENCE

Every living thing is of value in and of itself. Even those who take the lives of animals to use their bodies for human consumption can do so with reverence for the animal. It was customary in the practice of their spirituality for American Indians to pray for the spirit of the animal they killed and to thank it for giving up its life to sustain theirs.

When I was a lad in my early teens I began trapping muskrats and skunks for their pelts. Soon after I announced I was going to become a fur trapper, my father and later my grandfather came to me and said, "Bud, if you are going to trap that's well and good. But don't forget you still have your farm chores to do, and if you trap you must check your traps every morning and every evening. We won't tolerate animals having any more pain because you don't check your traps often."

If a person who does not have reverence becomes either angry or frustrated he or she is capable of great violence. We have experienced this in our society by wanton killing of innocent people. Many who have died at the hands of those who did not have reverence for life had nothing to do with creating the frustration that triggered the violence.

Adults teach reverence to children by their example. People who are taught reverence can suffer great frustration and still not do violent things to others. Without reverence frustrated children or adults can kill and justify the act in their minds. I am not saying that we should not spray the wasps on the porch, only that we should not put them to death without compassion and awareness that we are destroying life.

In some belief systems or societies one can say and truly mean, "With love and understanding I bless you on your path to your next higher lifetime." Maharish Mahesh Yogi, the seer who brought transcendental meditation to the West, sometimes reminded his students, "It is sometimes better to kill a cockroach than to disturb or stress the consciousness of a human." But dispatching even a cockroach was always to be done with awareness and love.

✧ TOLERANCE

The opposite of tolerance of course is intolerance. Intolerance is fear-based and born of ignorance. Intolerance leads to judgment. Judgment leads to prejudice. One of the great teachers of the twentieth century, psychologist Abraham Maslow wrote, "One of the least likely problems of a very mature person is racial, religious, ethnic, gender, or life-style prejudice."

Let us keep in mind, without prejudice there would be no wars. In all wars the enemy is depicted as sub-human. We could all significantly benefit from considering the precept that we are all one: *Anything I do for you, I do for me. Likewise, anything I do to you, I do to me.*

We can all start being increasingly tolerant by accepting that everyone is in the right place for him or her. We are all in different places, not right or wrong ones. When we accept where we are "at" we have taken the first step to preparing ourselves for growth that requires changing to another right place.

✧ HONESTY

We live in a society where lying is commonplace and

condoned. In our busy lives we often forget the simple truths that can carry us through tumultuous times. One such ancient truth is, *Truth sets you free*.

Sometimes truth is painful but we need to know that truth neither encumbers us nor entraps us. *Oh, what a tangled web we weave when first we practice to deceive*. It is important for us to realize this little ditty is indeed a truism.

The spiritual teacher Emmett Fox has defined wisdom as the perfect blending of intelligence (truth) and love. Intelligence or truth without love can be very cruel. Love without intelligence can be just as destructive. Consider the spoiled child.

Truth, even if painful, when blended with compassion is not of itself destructive and can strengthen the bonds of love and trust. Our quality of life is directly related to the level of trust and love characterizing our relationships.

To Help Us In The Process of Becoming

The idea of being clear on what kind of person I want to be is addressed elsewhere in this book. But being or becoming is worthy of additional consideration. I recommend that you take the few minutes necessary to find pen and paper and write out your answers to the following five questions. Your answers may help you in the process of moving toward what you want to become.

✦ What is the purpose of life in general?
✦ What is the purpose of my life?
✦ What do I want to become?
✦ What do I want to start doing to aid in my becoming?
✦ What do I want to stop doing?

If I have clarified who I want to be, I have a barometer that can be very useful. If I choose, I can review past behavior and learn from it. For example, I can examine a decision I made yesterday (or any time in the past) and ask, "Did that decision serve me well in view of what I now know and who I want to become?" If the answer to either part of this question is "no," then I have a clearer direction in terms of changing what I will do in a similar situation next time. Obviously the awareness of what I want to become is very useful when I am in the decision-making mode in the present tense.

Many of our great teachers have taught that you cannot know yourself too well. Let us now agree that while it is very important to know what and who we are now, it is equally important to be clear on who we want to become, which may indeed require *changing places.*

THE WORD FROM ABOVE

When I'm far from home and all alone
And know not what tomorrow holds,
Will my loved ones be safe when my day is done
And the last of the minutes is sold?

I am called to think of a philosopher's words
He will never receive his just due.
He didn't write during the time of the bard
And may not be included though his words be true.

He sat and thought and these words he did wrought.
"Each thing that I cherish it surely can perish"
And then he concluded as a landscape denuded,
"Everything that I own is a callable loan."

He sought far and wide for calmness inside.
What he sought for was cheer but he found only fear
And he waited inside for the pain to subside.
But the fears had their grip and caused tears.

Till he stumbled upon one word in the throng
Which could bury his fears from above
It's called love.

Chapter Three

OLD MESSAGES AND A NEW MESSENGER

Growth requires changing places—changing places may or may not be growth. To gain knowledge that clarifies and expands one's personal philosophy of life is to increase ones opportunities for growth.

Learning, joy, and happiness are sometimes found in strange places. If we limit our communications and our seeking to those with whom we share philosophy and beliefs we may be limiting out growth. It is the goal of this chapter to encourage the removal of spiritual blinders, even if temporarily.

I MADE THE FINAL READ-THROUGH of the final edit of the manuscript for the book, *You Are In The Right Place* in early November 1994. I looked at it one more time after the book designer had finished the layout and sent it off to the book manufacturer. The manuscript had been my constant companion, while at home and while traveling, for about twenty months.

Within a few days of mailing the manuscript I received a letter from a friend who had become a spiritual

mentor. In the letter he mentioned his excitement about a
trip he had planned for mid-December. He and several
other people would be returning to India to visit a swami
or holy man named Sathya Sai Baba.

I left within a week for a lecture engagement in
Portsmouth, Rhode Island, where I was to speak for a
day to the Rhode Island Dental Association. I was
excited about the trip, over and above my usual
enthusiasm, because of two things. Rhode Island was
one of only two states in the United States where I
had not lectured. Secondly, following the presentation, I would again return to a Maine hunting camp
where I would spend a week hunting white-tailed
deer with a group of very good friends. I had been
their guest twice before and twice they had been my
guests and hunted elk and deer with me in the Rocky
Mountains.

Hunting in the thickly timbered Maine woods is
very different from hunting in the wide-open spaces
of my beloved Rocky Mountains. The alone time in
nature, which I crave, is essentially the same. For
years hunting had been my opportunity for long, isolated meditations and uninterrupted opportunities to
talk to God. The Maine woods also provided this isolated privacy. I loved it.

For several years during many of my talks with
God, and always when I was hunting, I felt compelled
to ask the same question, "Should I remain a
hunter?" If God didn't want me to hunt I asked that
he give me a clear sign. Alone time in the wilderness
is also an opportunity to do my journaling, and I
always carry a note pad to record the events of the
day, my thoughts, and feelings.

The camaraderie in the Maine camp was delightful, even though the hunting was unproductive. My

journal entry on the last day contains what to me was a rather startling bit of information: During each of my three trips to this hunting camp, five to seven hunters had hunted five to seven full days. That totals more than ninety hunter days. The other hunters in this camp have hunted this same area for at least twenty years. All of them, in my opinion, are competent outdoorsmen and experienced hunters. And all except me had taken numerous deer while hunting here.

The strange awareness was that I realized that not one deer had ever been killed when I was in the camp. It would be typical for almost any camp with that many hunter days to average several deer each week. Additionally, I became aware of the fact that in the more than fifteen full days of hunting during my three visits, I had not seen even one deer. I am also an experienced hunter and a competent woodsman. I asked myself, "What's going on here?" I had a strong urge to visit with my spiritual mentor.

Shortly after I returned home I called him and we found a mutually acceptable time for a visit. I drove the two hours to his farm and after enjoying a Mexican food lunch we had a delightful afternoon of discussing spiritual philosophies and beliefs. When I brought up my concerns about being a hunter he asked me if it were a moral issue for me. I replied that I didn't think so, but it had begun to seem incongru-ent with where I was, and where I wanted to be spiri-tually. We both talked about other hunters we had known who are very spiritual men. I was pleased with the discussion, but it provided me with no answers.

Then I told him I was intrigued about his visit to India and Sai Baba. He responded by saying that since I had asked he would be happy to tell me about the swami. He talked in hushed tones about his experiences with Sai Baba and the messages of love he delivers daily to thousands of people from all over the world who travel to his ashram.

When I left a few hours later he gave me two cassette tapes recorded by Connie Shaw, a woman in the Denver area who had visited the swami many times. He also gave me a copy of *My Baba and I,* written by Dr. John Hislop.

In the next few days I listened to the entire set of tapes several times and read the book. What I read and heard was in many ways unsettling, and in other ways the most exciting information ever presented to me in my lifetime. The incredulity came from the statements that Sathya Sai Baba was, in the opinion of the writer and of the narrator, God incarnate, living in India at this time.

I have since watched several videotapes of the Swami and read a number of books about him. There are many witnessed accounts of him demonstrating his miraculous powers. I have interviewed about a dozen people who have witnessed his amazing feats. Such as, on several occasions, bringing dead people back to life and curing all manner of illnesses and physical deformities.

I also discovered that there are Sai Baba Centers in almost every large North American city. I visited one in Denver and one in the Fort Collins, Colorado area several times. They are invariably in someone's home. Sai Baba says, "Don't build buildings. Give that money to the poor." It was somewhat comforting to understand that Sai Baba was not asking for followers, or any kind of spiritual or religious conversion. His message is, "If you are a Christian, know and love Jesus with all your heart and your entire mind. If you are a Muslim, Hindu, a Jew, or a Buddhist, or of any other faith, afford your spiritual master nothing less."

I was also struck by another statement made by Connie Shaw: "If you ever meet anyone who is raising money for Sai Baba you know immediately the person is a fraud. Sai Baba has no fund raising."

I discussed my introduction to Sai Baba with one of my daughters, her husband, and a teenaged grandson. I showed them the book *My Baba and I.* My son-in-law instantly recognized a picture of Sai Baba as one he had seen in the home of a family he knew who had emigrated from India. A few weeks later we enjoyed dinner with that family at my daughter's home.

The faces of the man and his wife fairly beamed when I started asking questions about Sai Baba. They knew him well. He had officiated at their wedding and named two of their three daughters. They openly discussed the many miracles and healings of the sick they had seen him perform. They discussed the fine, fragrant gray ash, called *vibhutti,* which he produces from his fingertips. It is often used in the same manner as holy water in the Catholic Church, and in healing the seriously ill.

The discussion about the healing gray ash prompted me to tell them about my great concern for my seven-month-old grandson who had been frequently hospitalized, and was in fact in the hospital at that time. My concern was greatly heightened because of the concern of the physicians who attended the baby. They seemed unable to reverse the dehydration of his tiny body. My newfound friends suggested I follow them to their home and they would give me a packet of *vibhutti*. I did so and then went directly to the hospital.

It was midnight when I arrived at the hospital. My distraught and sleepy daughter did not know how to respond as I prayed the words "aum-sai-ram" as instructed by my new friend. I then sprinkled the *vibhutti* on the chest and back of the feverish, whimpering baby. My grandson was released from the hospital a few days later. He had several other bouts with a strange digestive malady and allergic reactions to almost all foods. Today, as this is being written, he is a healthy, happy, redheaded bundle of energy, and even at this early age he is a phenomenal athlete.

Another Hunt

That autumn my wife left the day after Thanksgiving on a business trip that would keep her away for about a week. My work was caught up and there were reports that the goose and duck hunting were very good in southeastern Colorado.

That prompted me to pack my truck for the three-hour ride to a hunting club of which I was a member. There were eleven other members. I liked all of them and some were dear friends.

Thanksgiving weekend is traditionally the busiest weekend of the year at the club. I eagerly looked forward to a weekend of camaraderie, jokes and laughter, good whiskey and sport.

I arrived at the clubhouse too late for the evening hunt and was quite surprised that none of my friends was there. I prepared my supper and enjoyed a quiet evening of reading and meditation, all the while expecting other hunters to arrive at any time. None came.

I arose the next morning almost two hours before daylight and enjoyed coffee and a good breakfast. I then departed for my favorite goose pit in plain sight of the lake on which about two thousand geese were resting. I was in place before daylight, which prevented the geese from seeing me, and I eagerly awaited the first flight of the big birds.

Solitude always prompts me to talk to God and this time was no different. After the usual "check in," and thanking him for the privilege of being there, I again asked if I should continue to hunt. If he responded to my question I missed it. A few minutes later the first flock of about 100 Canada geese arose from the lake and flew low directly toward my pit. I waited until they were within easy range, took careful aim at a large goose, and was surprised when it didn't instantly fall from my first shot. But no matter, I squeezed off the second shot. I missed again. I quickly reloaded my double-barreled shotgun and had another easy target, a low-flying straggler. Strangely, it was even closer. I took my time, and I missed with both barrels again. I'm not a great shotgunner, but I am competent, and I could hardly believe I missed four easy shots.

I knew that no other geese were likely to fly over the pit I was in and decided to walk about a half-mile to another pit, which was well concealed. I was walking by some large posts used to support a corner in a pasture fence when I saw another flock of geese flying directly toward me. I leaned up against a large post for concealment. It worked. The geese were flying right over me as I released the safety on my shotgun and took careful aim. To my chagrin the gun would not fire. I hurriedly checked the safety and again took aim and tried to fire a second time. And still my prized shotgun, which had served me so perfectly in the past, would not fire.

The geese were well out of range when I checked the safety the third time. I pointed the gun skyward, pulled the trigger, and both barrels fired perfectly. I continued my walk to the pit and was seated comfortably inside when I began reviewing the events of the last hour. A few minutes later I left the pit and walked back to the clubhouse. I spent the day reading and

A MOUNTAIN MAN WOULD I BE

(A Clair audio message received by author La Corriere, 1995)

There are lots of mountains
and
there always will be.

There are lots of men
and
there always will be.

There are lots of men in those mountains
and
there always will be.

But there will not always be a lot of Mountain Men.

❖ ❖ ❖

So what is a Mountain Man?

He lives by his code—
He walks his talk.
He says what he'll do and does not balk.

napping and talking to God. I also took a long ride in
my truck looking at the abandoned homesteads pecu-
liar to the area with their strange stone buildings.

The next morning I awoke again well before daylight and cooked a big breakfast. I had no desire to
hunt. Instead, I eagerly washed the dishes, tidied up
the clubhouse and packed my truck. I left two days
earlier than I had planned for the long drive to my
daughter's house to see my new granddaughter for
the first time.

A Change in Perspective

Several months earlier I had made a commitment
to another group for a hunt. This was a multi-game
hunt in extreme south Texas. It would have been
quite awkward to cancel at this late date and I decided to keep the commitment. I also decided I would
attempt to hunt as enthusiastically as I had in previous years and then perhaps I could decide whether I
would become an ex-hunter.

During the first morning out I shot at and missed a
large white-tailed buck. Incidentally, I am an excellent
marksman with a rifle. Later in the day when we were
to hunt quail the wind blew such a gale that hunting
was impossible. I was relieved. The following day of
turkey hunting was unproductive. We saw no birds.

On the last evening of the hunt I was in a deer stand
and watched two groups of three deer each for almost an
hour. I knew that I must shoot soon or the descending
darkness would make it impossible. I recalled my decision
to hunt "with enthusiasm" and finally decided to shoot
the middle deer in one of the groups.

I was nearly ready to squeeze off the shot when I
experienced a painful cramping of the muscles on my
right side. That seemed strange—I had never had a

cramp on the side of my rib cage before. I didn't think there were any muscles there to cramp! I set the rifle aside and rubbed out the cramp.

As soon as I was comfortable again I picked up the rifle, took careful aim, and fired. The deer died instantly from the well-placed bullet. I experienced a tremendous sigh of relief. Now, I know the relief was for two reasons: the animal died instantly, and as I removed the spent cartridge from my rifle I knew I had made a decision to become an ex-hunter. For the next six years I did not pick up a rifle or a shotgun.

Since then I have been on several bird hunts. I hunted pheasants in western Nebraska and bobwhite quail in south Texas. I fully enjoyed both outings and blessed the spirits of each bird that I killed. Later, as table fare, they were delicious.

It is a bit difficult for me to explain why my willingness to end the life of another of God's creatures has reverted to my cultural roots. I'm convinced that knowing that there is no death, for the animal whose life I take, or for myself, is a part of it. Perhaps increased spiritual understanding has removed any guilt I might have previously experienced as a hunter. I have only a few regrets in my life but none for the years I spent as an ex-hunter, and none for resuming the activity.

More Lifestyle Changes

For several years I have enjoyed one week each fall with my close friend Jim, roaming the back country mountains of Colorado in my four-wheel drive truck. Our main activity is fly-fishing for trout. We have labeled our week N.A.W.—No Agenda Week.

Feeding trout are most active about one hour before sunset to about one hour after. Our typical day would end well after dark as we prepared our large

evening meal and ate around a campfire. One
evening, as we stumbled around in the shadowy light
of the campfire preparing dinner, we concluded that
we would be much better off having our main meal at
noon when the trout seem to take a nap, and cook a
much simpler meal at night. We started the next day.

After several days of our new regimen, we both
commented on how much better we slept, and how
much better we felt in the mornings. Our evening
meals consisted almost entirely of canned vegetables
and fresh fruit.

At that time my family and I lived in the country
and for years I had a large and very productive veg-
etable garden. The dietary experience while camping
prompted me on several different occasions to restrict
my food intake to vegetables and fruit for several
days at a time. I liked the more alert or less sluggish
feeling the vegetarian diet gave me.

I hadn't even remotely considered doing anything
about becoming a vegetarian, even after reading
books about Sai Baba. However, his teaching is very
clear, "We shouldn't eat our friends, the animals."

A few months after being introduced to the swami
one of my dear and respected friends wrote me a letter about how excited he was about a vegetarian diet
he had started. He told me in glowing terms of the
huge drop in his cholesterol and of the pounds that
just melted away. I rationalized, "But Randy gets
excited about a lot of things!" That is one of my
friend's wonderful traits.

Still, more months passed. One day, on a long road
trip with my friend Dennis, we listened to several
hours of tapes by Randy's dietary mentor. Dennis
hadn't discounted our mutual friend's letter! By the
time our road trip was over I was convinced I should

give a fair trial to the diet, which eliminates all animal products, including dairy. I remained true to a vegan diet (no animal products) for more than two years. My cholesterol did drop but my weight did not.

During that same two-year period I also decided to stop drinking alcohol. I was somewhat concerned that it might be as difficult as stopping smoking had been for me many years before. To my relief I had no difficulty whatsoever. I wanted to know if abstinence would have a noticeable effect on my daily functioning. My observation is that the effects were negligible.

I'm glad I gave myself the experience of being a vegetarian and being alcohol-free but also glad I am again enjoying steaks, seafood, good wine, and martinis. Being temperate seems to suit my temperament.

TO BE EMPOWERED

Sometimes things do go well for me,
At others I have to try.
Sometimes my confidence is all I see,
At others I almost cry.

Frustration and fear, the failure twins
Try to get hold of me.
At times like this the human will
Speaks louder than before.
But there's a stronger vice still,
Just inside our door

We hear it not when blinded by fear,
Listening is the key.
For fearful hearts have weak ears,
Or so it seems to me.

Chapter Four

HELLO! IS ANYONE HOME?

**It has been widely taught that every problem
contains the seeds to it solution. To change
our behavior, and thus our life's circumstances,
always begins in our mind—our thinking. If we
are experiencing undesirable circumstances,
and if our thinking leads us away from personal
responsibility for our current situation, the only
alternative is "victim hood." Problems and pain
are an inevitable and integral part of life. Being
the victim of our problems, just as with suffering
from our pain, is always a choice. It is the purpose of this chapter to enhance the acceptance
of the personal power to make positive changes
in our circumstances that is inherent in every
human being.**

F OR MANY YEARS MY FAMILY AND FRIENDS have kindly
tolerated another of my many idiosyncrasies—
being mentally absent while being physically present.
Any time I would become disinterested with the conversation of the moment (i.e. bored!) my habit was to
take myself on a mental journey to a more satisfying
or entertaining place and/or activity.

For many years, and from many sources, I have
received the teaching that emphasizes the importance

of living totally in the "here and now." In my opinion one of the great teachers of the twentieth century was Mahatma Gandhi, who taught, "For heaven's sake, wherever you are, be there!"

In spite of my awareness I allowed this mind-wandering and deluded myself into thinking this was a beneficial anomaly. I suspect this behavior may be quite common. For many years I accepted the notion that life is a school. With that line of thinking our task is to grow toward perfection by becoming aware of our imperfections and overcoming them. In recent years, from the information I have gained from books on quantum physics and other sources, I have changed my thinking. First, we must discover and accept who we are as God's child. If we do so life can become a process of creating the life we want to lead.

This line of thinking, tracks with the concept of universal mind, which holds that we already know everything. The concept of universal mind is sometimes referred to as "infinite intelligence" and by at least one scientist/philosopher, Walter Russell, as "the universal knowledge bank." Russell believed the way to access this information is through meditation.

Dr. Albert Einstein also supported this theory. Einstein said that he was uncomfortable accepting the accolades for his discoveries. His comments suggested that the information that enabled his discoveries was available to everyone.

This philosophy suggests that *if we seek this knowledge* we will be presented with repeated opportunities to rediscover what we already know at a non-conscious level. However, we may choose to pursue, or not to pursue, this information and use it in creative ways.

Further, it is important for us to realize that we are not given a problem just to solve it. Our more important task is to discover the reason behind the problem, or why we experienced the problem in the first place. Until we discover this we will find ourselves solving the same problem over and over again. It can become a cruel, repetitious bore. When we do experience the same problem repeatedly our humanness makes us susceptible to thinking of ourselves as victims and asking, "Why me, Lord?"

In recent years such highly respected authors as Larry Dossey, Fritjof Capra, Gary Zukov, Deepak Chopra and Wayne Dyer have written a lot about quantum physics. They, and the other previously mentioned thought leaders, (philosopher Walter Russell and scientist Albert Einstein) support the concept that all information or intelligence is contained in one "repository."

Quantum physicists also tell us that not only do all of us have this ability, but even more shocking, that we already possess all knowledge and information. Our task is to remove the blockages that render us incapable of tapping into this infinite resource. In this scenario our task is not to learn, or gain information, it is to unblock the hidden or blocked channels and allow us the ability to remember the information and knowledge already in our possession. Perhaps most importantly we need to remember who we are—God's children, created in his image and likeness.

Because of who we are it is important to accept as part of our reality that we are also creators. Consider how different our lives would be if we began each day by excitedly saying, "What wonderful things can I create today with God's help?" Compare that approach to sitting on our hands and thinking, "I wonder what things will come my way today?" For several years I said with all of the conviction and commitment of which I was capable, "God, just tell me what you want me to do and I shall give it my very best shot." Things started picking up in my life in terms of fulfilling my desires when I adopted a different communication pattern. I now believe all the time I was saying, "What do you want me to do, God?" God was trying to say to me, *"What do you want to do, Bud? I'll help you."* And I wasn't listening.

This is further acceptance and utilization of one of God's most accepted promises—*"I give you free will on which I never impinge."* We accept that God has given us free will. But what free will do I have if God is telling me what to do? Oh, I can tell you, I really wanted God to tell me what to do. Then I would not be responsible! But I must be responsible if I am to fulfill my responsibilities to my family, fellow human beings, my God, and myself.

Attempting to Tap Universal Knowledge

As with many people who grew up in poverty during the Great Depression, I have fought "poverty thinking" throughout my adult life. In my young and formative years every time I heard my parents talking about money it was always in a negative light. The discussions always gave me a fearful feeling. I learned at an early age to avoid thinking about money more than was absolutely necessary. I carried this behavior, this learned way of avoiding that which I remembered as painful, into adulthood. As a consequence I avoided all but the most necessary involvement with the financial activities of my life.

Then one day, as I was reluctantly wrestling with a particularly stressful financial problem, I realized I had been violating one of my own teachings, which is, *we will be given repeated opportunities to learn a particular lesson, but whether we learn the lesson or not is a choice.* Additionally, as stated earlier, it is important for us to understand that we are not given a problem merely to solve it. To be rid of the problem, we must also understand what created the problem in the first place—in this instance, poverty thinking.

For all those years I had chosen to withdraw from the discomfort of financial affairs and not be present, I thus greatly reduced the possibility of discovering a better way to handle financial matters. Becoming fully aware that "I cannot give from empty pockets" helped me make a change. With this realization I committed to never again avoid my financial responsibilities. I now have a feeling of current and future prosperity I have never experienced before.

The change in behavior was certainly progress. But it did not address another critical factor—the nature of my thinking. One book that succinctly addresses this is *As a Man Thinketh,* written in 1906 by James Allen. The ready availability of this book, almost 100 years after it was written, attests to its usefulness.

If you choose to read Allen's book (it can be read in an evening) I'm sure you will find as I, and millions of others have, that the concept is sound. Many of the leading thinkers of our time, including Norman Vincent Peale, (author of *The Power of Positive Thinking)* advocating self-determination by governing our thoughts have "stood on the shoulders" of Allen.

Deepak Chopra and Wayne Dyer have been instrumental in expanding this principle to include what is now referred to *as the law of attraction.* This law holds that we attract circumstances to ourselves from one of two sources—those things we love, or those we fear or hate. What we attract, to ourselves is not controlled by that which we want, but that which we think!

A Test to Prove Thoughts Have Energy—
Woo Woo Wands

It is helpful if we can accept that thoughts are "things"—and that they have measurable energy. The nature of the energy of our thoughts can raise us to higher levels of thinking and being, or can drag us down to the depths of despair and depression.

There is a highly reliable method that will prove to skeptics that thoughts do indeed have measurable energy. To build a very simple "energy meter" straighten two wire clothes hangars, bend them into an L shape with a 6 inch handle and an 18 inch wand. Place a drinking straw on the handle so the wand can be held, one in each hand, and swing freely. You may hold the wands yourself or have someone else hold them, and it isn't necessary for that person to know what you are testing.

Have the person hold the wands level, about chest high, with their hands about 8 inches apart. As soon as the wands have stopped jiggling ask the holder to think about how she or he felt when they saw the World Trade Center towers fall. The wands will slowly but surely cross. Instruct the person to lay the wands down, shake off the negative energy and pick the wands up again. This time, when the wands have settled down, have the person think about someone they dearly love, such a spouse, a child, a best friend or parent. As if by magic the wands will maximally separate!

We have long known about the cause of psycho-somatic illness—created by thinking negative thoughts of sickness. One more time—we attract to ourselves not that which we want, but that which we think most about! Negative thinking about money is no different! I wanted prosperity, but every time I thought about money it was tied to my old pain. I don't want pain! For me to become prosperous it was necessary for me to stop thinking of money as a painful and necessary evil, and to start thinking about it as something good—something I appreciate. It took awhile, but along with the gift of a generous friend, I changed the quality of my thinking, focusing my thought energy on *what I wanted,* rather than on circumstances I didn't want.

Our thoughts are "mental currency" with which we "purchase" our future. What happened as a result of my change in thinking validated what I have long believed: *We are totally in charge of our own destinies.* Tapping into the universal knowledge bank begins by taking small steps and proving to ourselves that we are not *powerless,* but *powerful.*

Other Benefits of Being Present

A Course in Miracles teaches that when I am totally present, I draw closer to the brother or sister I am with, and closer to God. When I distance myself from another person, I also distance myself from God. Any activity that distances me from God is antithetical to my major purpose in life, which is to do everything I can to know truth, and God, and fulfill my mission.

In Deepak Chopra's newsletter, *Namaste,* he tells us to remind ourselves:

> *I am tuned in—fully awake—fully present—*
> *giving full attention to the people I am with*
> *at this moment.*

Motivation to Change Places to Another Right Place

For many of us growth is so often "three steps forward and two steps back." Unfortunately sometimes it seems we take three steps forward and slide back

three. **We may think there is no gain, but let us
not undervalue the experience.** Often we think of
growth as difficult and perhaps even painful, and we
have all heard about how natural it is for human
beings to resist change for ego-based (that is fear-
based) reasons. It may well be normal to resist change,
but it is not natural. What is normal is that which is
customary in our society. What is natural is what love
would have us do, for that is what we are. That often
requires change and working through our fear.

If we convince ourselves that change is difficult it
is much more likely to **be** difficult, and we may never
make the commitment to attempt planned, beneficial
change. This is particularly true if the change we
have in mind requires discipline. We must be ever
mindful that change for ego-based reasons is change
that is motivated by fear. It is indeed to our benefit to
remember that if we make fear-based decisions we
shall live with more fear in our lives and, as a natural
result, less happiness.

Fear and love are opposites. If fear dominates our
lives, love is minimized and so is happiness. Our
decision making determines which emotion will control us—If you make more fear-based decisions, you
will live with more fear. Keep in mind that you cannot be happy and afraid at the same time. If the motivation to change is spiritually based, that is, love-
based, we have a completely different set of dynam-
ics going for us. God's promise is that He will provide
all the energy and the resources necessary for us to
accomplish our deepest love-based desires. But the
choice is ours. The following parable can help us
clarify the simplicity of choosing our own future:

An old American Indian was teaching his grandson about life. "A fight is going on inside me," he said to the boy. "It is a terrible fight and it is between two wolves. One is evil—he is anger, hatred, envy, sorrow, regret, greed, arrogance, self-pity, guilt, resentment, inferiority, lies, false pride, superiority, and ego. The other is good— he is joy, peace, love, hope, serenity, humility, kindness, benevolence, empathy, generosity, truth, compassion, and faith.

The same fight is going on inside you—and every other person.

The grandson thought about it and then asked the grandfather, "Which wolf will win?"

The old Indian replied simply, "The one you feed."

HOW CAN I HELP

I remember September Morning Promise
And doubt that I can ever capture,
Again the words and put them down,
The surrender of sweet sorrow's rapture.
So dear

But if I can, may it be now
While desire is at my centre,
To quote a wiser One than me,
And give to all who choose to enter.
Without fear

Into life's main stream, though it be rough,
I choose to risk my self-content.
To know the joy the cost is dear
But I shall gladly pay without portent.
Of fear

It's here, right now and all around
It's vibrant and alive,
Can I share my gift with others?
I'm damned that I shall try

I'll share with all my strength
If only one can see, with me
And hear

[September Morning Promise—a poem written earlier by the author]

Chapter Five

TURNING POINTS

One beautiful Indian summer day, when I was a small boy of nine or ten years, Grandma Ham and I were sitting on her porch in rocking chairs. Our family had recently undergone a family crisis. In her best story-telling style she told me, *"Buddy, life is like a mountain river, sometimes is runs still and smooth, deep and peaceful. But you can be sure that downstream a bit there will be rapids and perhaps even falls. And then it will smooth out again for a time. Our challenge is to accept whatever conditions the river of life hands us, doing our best and always knowing we are never left alone and comfortless by our Creator. We should always remember—this too shall pass."*

The purpose of this chapter is to help you develop a useful perspective of the many turning points each of us experience in life as Godsends and greet them with greater equanimity

I T IS QUITE POSSIBLE that our perception about our quality of life depends on acceptance of the philosophical position that each of us is, at any given time in our lives, in exactly the right place. Before anecdotally exploring the validity of the concept let us consider two of its main components:

> • To quote Ekhart Tolle, author of *The Power of Now,* when considering any evolving situation, whether we like it or abhor it, *"It is as it is."* In this context you are where you are, you can be no place else!
>
> • Lesson #193 in *A Course in Miracles— Workbook* is: *All things are lessons God would have me learn.* **If we can accept all events, especially undesirable ones, as learning opportunities we can view them in a totally different light.**

One of the great thinkers, teachers and philosophers of the last century was psychologist Dr. Carl Rogers who crafted the Learning Ladder. The concept describes a step-by-step process that can help us to take successful action to change an unwanted habit or behavior.

The process always begins with our awareness and ownership of a problem *and* a desire to change. "Awareness" is the first rung on the ladder—it is "where I am at." Until we accept our current circumstances it is difficult, if not impossible, to move **to another more desirable right place.** This movement constitutes growth.

About thirty years ago author Gail Sheehy wrote the best selling book *Passages.* She and I are probably addressing the same category of life experiences. I refer to these life events as Turning Points.

At this time in my life (approaching 73 years of age) I may not yet be in the final chapter of my life's work, but I'm certainly not in an early chapter! As I look back on the pervious chapters it seems that there has been a stream of events that have contributed to the fulfilling successes I have enjoyed as a self-proclaimed "T O G" (Teacher of God). [*In A Course in Miracles* Jesus tells us that *"All are called but few accept the responsibility."*] I now choose to think of these incidents (turning points) as Divine Interventions. Yet, at the time they happened it was impossible for me to see any pattern or benefit. I could not have foreseen that the events would even be useful, let alone eventually prove essential and therefore priceless, in preparing me for a career that has been my passion for more than thirty-five years.

The stream of events began before my teenage years when I was in elementary school. The sequence of events is as follows:

✧ DEPARTED THE ACADEMIC PATH OF BEING AN EXCELLENT STUDENT (THE FIRST FOUR YEARS) AND I BECAME A POOR ONE.

- When I was eleven years old I had a serious kidney infection and missed the first five weeks of school. It was customary at that time for one teacher to be with each grade for the entire school year—our class had five substitute teachers who rotated in and out. When scoring test papers the teachers had us exchange papers with another student—I always exchanged with Donald Goss— we always gave each other a good grade. I was just getting a glimmer of understanding on how to do long division when the class moved on to decimals. I never caught up in math or the other subjects and began seeing myself as a slow learner.

✧ DEVELOPING A PASSIONATE LOVE OF THE FIELD SPORTS OF FISHING, TRAPPING AND HUNTING.

• I started fishing when I was six, trapping and hunting when I was twelve. Neither of my parents finished the eighth grade—they paid little attention to my school work but insisted that I must graduate high school. They praised me mightily for my out-of-doors skills.

✧ THE BIRTH OF A PHYSICALLY DISABLED BROTHER.

• I was twelve when my brother Dan was born. It wasn't long before we knew he was "crippled." Of course now we use the words "physically challenged" or disabled. At the time physicians said he was "spastic." It was years later before we heard the term cerebral palsy. In the mid-1940s it was common for such children to be kept isolated from the public. My mother would not allow that—Danny was with us wherever we went. My pain became significantly greater after hearing an Evangelist Baptist preacher proclaim that "The sins of the fathers shall be visited upon the heads of the children until the seventh generation." Until then I was proud of my heritage as a member a totally honorable family—after that sermon I had grave doubts. My feelings of self-worth plunged.

✧ MY FATHER'S INFIDELITY.

• This happened about a year after Dan's birth. It lasted only a year but was a severe blow to my already weakened self-esteem. My immature pride and unforgivness kept us from being friends for 23 years.

✧ Being thrust into a position of responsibility and leadership in high school.

• In high school it was well known that I was a poor student who took "snap courses" but that I was "a good, hard working kid." One of the snap courses I took as a Junior and Senior was wood working. In the small town high school at Florence, Colorado even the Principal was required to teach at least two, hour-long classes. Our Principal, Mr. Brenton, called me into his office on the first day of my senior year. He told me he needed help and would like me to "be in charge" of the two after-noon shop classes. He told me that if I would do that I would not have to worry about having all the credits I needed to graduate—I accepted. It was a tremendous challenge; Mr. Brenton never visited the class during the entire year. I doubt that the students learned very much, but I did maintain a semblance of orderliness and no one lost a finger to a power saw or had other injuries.

✧ Enlisting in the United States Marine Corps.

• A complete essay on this turning point is con-tained in my book You are in *The Right Place*. The short version is that my friend Jimmy talked me into joining the military during the Korean War, shortly after I graduated high school. Jimmy didn't pass the entrance exams. In retrospect it is easy for me to see the importance of this turning point— perhaps one of the most important in my life.

✧ Appointment to leadership positions in the Marines.

• At eighteen months into my enlistment I was promoted from PFC to Corporal, a normal event. Shortly thereafter I was assigned to be the only

Drill Instructor for 75 marines who had just completed boot camp and were assigned to advanced combat training. They severely challenged my authority but I successfully overcame the challenge. I was nineteen years old.

✧ Turning points leading to a twenty year career in the Bell Telephone System.

• At the time of my discharge from the Marines the Captain I reported told me I was a good man and he was sorry I had chosen not to reenlist. He presented me with sealed envelope with a man's name on it. He said, "Corporal Ham as you go back home to Colorado visit the Standard Oil Field Office in Grand Junction, give this letter to this man and he will give you a job—not a dead end job—a job with a future."

• On a Sunday afternoon in mid-May two recently discharged buddies and I were driving through central Arizona toward the Four Corners area. On Monday we planned a stop in Grand Junction in the southwest part of the state where I would, in all probability, accept my new job. A newscast on the car radio informed us that there was a serious spring snowstorm in the Four Corners area and all roads were blocked—travelers were advised to avoid the area. We turned east at Gallop, New Mexico to enter Colorado through the southeast corner of the state. I was very disappointed.

• I arrived home in Southeastern Colorado with no money and no car. I went back to work for the construction company I worked for when I joined the Marines. I planned to go to Grand Junction as soon as I had a little money and a car. The construction company was involved in a mountain water diversion project. I had two close calls with death from dynamite explosions in the first week. Since I had survived the Marines I decided not to stick around for three! I quit. The boss said he would mail me my check. A fellow construction worker agreed to give me a ride to the mountain town of Salida, Colorado where I could catch a bus home if I would give him a couple of dollars for gas. The bus would arrive at a neighboring town about nine miles from my home at 1:00 AM. After paying for the ticket and calling my father to meet the bus I had fifty cents left. While waiting for my bus I joined a conversation with five other men— they were older—maybe thirty. They were on their way to the Elephant Buttes dam building project in Southern New Mexico and told me they needed another dump-truck driver. They said don't worry about money—they would cover me until payday. There was only one problem left— I was twenty-five cents short of having enough money to call my father back so he wouldn't meet the bus. Somehow I couldn't ask them to loan me a quarter. Two days later I went to work for the telephone company. I spent the next twenty years as an employee of the Bell System. I never went to Grand Junction. That summer I met my first wife, we were married one year later.

✧ THRUST INTO LEADERSHIP ROLES AS A TELEPHONE LINEMAN.

• A telephone lineman's job is physically demanding and climbing poles was just dangerous enough to make it exciting. I loved it and I became quite competent. One day I had a misunderstanding that resulted in a strong "nose-to-nose" confrontation with the line foreman—a crusty old-timer. At a crew meeting that Friday after work, rather than transferring me to another crew (which I fully expected), he announced to the other five linemen that henceforth, when he wasn't on the job site, I was in charge. I was the youngest man on the crew by several years. After the first week of being tested by the crew we got along fine. The boss was increasingly absent, on most days we saw him only at the beginning and at days end.

✧ BECOMING A STUDENT AGAIN AT 27 YEARS OF AGE.

• My next assignment was a promotion from the roving line crew to Combinationman. As the title implies there was a wide variety of responsibilities including repairing and building telephone lines; repairing telephone instruments; maintaining central office equipment; patrolling long-distance toll lines on the mountain passes around Salida, Colorado and a myriad of other duties.

• One afternoon my manager came to me and told me that an adult education class was coming to town and he invited me to go with him to the demonstration meeting. The demonstration was on the Dale Carnegie Human Relations Course. The course was held one night a week for fourteen weeks. The cost was $160.00. At the time I had a wife and baby daughter; a house mortgage; a car payment and all of the other attendant expenses; and I was earning $55.00 per week. I went to the bank and borrowed the money. That $160 has been returned to me actually thousands of times! Because of this course I became a continuous student—I obtained a library card and joined The Book of the Month Club. As a direct result of this course I became a public speaker. I could not possibly have chosen a better investment of my money, time and energy.

✧ IN MY NEWLY ACCEPTED ROLE OF CONTINUOUS STUDENT I WAS INTRODUCED TO BOOKS ABOUT THE PROPHET OF VIRGINIA BEACH, EDGAR CAYCE.

• The book *Great Religions by which Men Live*, and subsequent study in paranormal psychology profoundly changed my life.

✧ PROMOTION TO A WHITE COLLAR JOB—TELEPHONE BUSINESS SALES.

• My newfound enthusiasm as a student paved the way for me to be selected from twenty applicants for a sales position in Colorado Springs. I was interviewed by three mid-level executives. One of the questions they asked was, "What have you read recently?" I answered, *"War and Peace; Many Mansions; The Red Badge of Courage; and To Kill a Mockingbird."* A year earlier and I would have answered, "The Denver Post and Outdoor Life!"

• Until that time in my Bell System Career my performance reviews could have been considered outstanding. If at any time I felt my rating might be slipping I could always bring it up by just working harder. I found that working harder as a salesman was not producing the desired results. My first performance review as a salesman was scheduled at the end of six months. I knew my performance was mediocre at best. Sales performance can be measured to the penny and my results fell short of expected levels three of the first six months. I entered my sales manager's office for the review with great trepidation. I feared that I might be demoted to a technical job wherein I had had high ratings.

• My sales manager put me at ease with his first statement. He said, "Bud I believe you have a brilliant future with the Bell System and I want to do all I can to have that happen sooner rather than later." I could tell by his body language, his choice of words, tone of voice, and his facial expressions that I was in a safe place. I spent the next hour intently listening and absorbing everything he said. During that time he gave me five suggestions for improving my sales results. *Not one criticism—five relevant suggestions*. I never received my one year review. In a few months my results were off the charts and I was promoted to Exchange Manager in eastern Colorado.

✧ PROMOTED TO AN IDEAL MANAGERIAL POSITION.

• The manager I replaced may not have been incompetent but he was at least inept—it would have been difficult for me to fail. I retained my rating of outstanding performance. I relished the responsibilities of being the manager of 40 people.

✧ PROMOTED TO MANAGEMENT TRAINER.

• Three years later I was again promoted. My new title was Personnel Staff Supervisor with the assignment of conducting management training classes. I could not have been more pleased and excited. In this new position I was expected to read books on management sciences, communications, psychology and personal growth. I devoured them as if they were delightful novels.

• A requirement of my new assignment was my participation in a two-week training retreat at

Mount Pocono Inn in Pennsylvania. The event was called "T" Group. Each group of twelve participants was facilitated by specially trained Fellows from the National Training Laboratories at Bethel, Maine. The activity was a nearly total immersion in self-awareness. It was a life altering experience. As with all personal growth experiences, all of the news wasn't good news—I received reinforcing feedback about my leadership skills but also that I was judgmental and sympathy-seeking!

✧ APPOINTED TO THE POSITION OF ORGANIZATION DEVELOPMENT SPECIALIST AND IN-COMPANY MANAGEMENT CONSULTANT IN MOUNTAIN BELL TELEPHONE.

• I was in "the right place at the right time." The end of my two-year, rotational assignment as a management trainer coincided perfectly with the decision by AT&T and the Bell System to experiment with in-company management consultants in connection with an Organization Development Program. For the next several years I would describe my learning curve as the steepest I ever experienced. I was totally committed to becoming a competent consultant but I had no mentor or model, and no peer with whom to share successes and failures. The work became my mission and my passion and slowly I became more competent. Small successes became major sources of motivation. The greatest highlight of this assignment was when I was selected by AT & T to be an assistant trainer at a "T" Group at Mount Pocono Inn. As I grew busier a second consultant was assigned as an understudy to help me.

✧ COMMITTING CORPORATE [PROMOTIONAL] SUICIDE.
   • The Assistant Vice President to whom I reported as
O. D. Specialist was not totally supportive of my role.
He was "old-school" and an authoritarian. He considered my work as a bit "touchy-feely." In the personnel department that he headed there were five
sub-departments—mine being one of them. One day
as I was in his office on a routine matter he said,
"Bud, I understand from other department heads that
you have done a management analysis for them and
they have found it to be useful. Why don't you tell
me how our department is doing?" It was nearly
noon and I had a full afternoon of appointments so
we agreed to meet the following morning at 11:00
and I would give him my report after which we
would go to lunch. I knew this was my big chance
but I quickly decided to tell him as honestly and
compassionately as I could my honest evaluation of
the other four sub-departments. I determined I would
offer him at least one recommendation for each defi-
ciency I identified. The problem was that there were
many deficiencies—we were often the laughing stock
of the company and it was well known that his management style was antithetical to the teaching and
purposes of the Organization Development Program.
After my presentation we did not go to lunch, yet I
still held out hope he would find my feedback useful.
It was a forlorn hope!
   • The day following my report presentation the
new consultant I was mentoring came bursting
into our office and excitedly told me that our boss
had asked him to do a through evaluation of the
department and report to him in three days. He
was not aware of my report. The young man said,
"You know Bud, this is my big chance." I agreed

with him that it was. One week later he was promoted to the next management level and I was
laterally transferred to another department.
• In the next few months there were three upper-
management positions that became available. I
was arguably the best qualified person for each of
those promotions but I wasn't contacted. I called
one of the Assistant Vice Presidents and asked
him what was going on. He told me that my for-
mer boss, the Personnel Vice President, had let it
be known as long as he held his position I would
not be promoted—he had iron clad authority. It
was then I decided that as soon as I had vested
rights in the pension plan I would resign and
become an independent management consultant.

✧ MEETING AND FALLING IN LOVE WITH MY WIFE OF THIRTY-
THREE YEARS.

• My new assignment (after committing corporate
suicide) was enjoyable and challenging. I was
Traffic Chief for long-distance telephone operators
for one-half of the Denver area. I had five-hundred,
eighty employees in my organization. This was
before direct distance dialing and most of the
employees were women. One of the Chief Operators
became my present wife of thirty-three years on the
last day of my employment in the Bell System.

✧ THIRTY-THREE YEARS OF BEING A FREE-LANCE CONSULTANT.

• I had planned my departure from the Bell
System for about two years before leaving and
took advantage of every opportunity to become
known as a consultant in the Denver community.
At that time there was a non-profit organization in
Denver called the Adult Education Council. It was

supported by voluntary contributions from local businesses and their mission was to provide low cost communications and personal growth retreats for employees of the Council's sponsors. I became active as a trainer in the Council during my tenure as an in-company consultant. Through that activity I met Dr. Alton Barbour and two other professors from Denver University. We became good friends and decided we would start our own organization to conduct personal growth retreats. We named our organization The Rocky Mountain Behavioral Institute. The four of us conducted live-in personal growth retreats on a regular basis for several years. Working closely with three PhDs provided a tremendous source of learning for me. My self-worth as an educator and student took a great leap forward when my three associates decided I should the Director of our institute.

• My exposure to the larger business community was greatly enhanced by these personal growth retreats. My colleagues and I advertised to the business community and our first retreat was fully subscribed and among those attending were two dentists, Sam and Jim, with whom I have had a relationship for more than thirty years—the Callender brothers. They also have two other brothers—all four brothers are orthodontists. I became a consultant to brother Sam's practice. After several team building sessions with Sam's staff several other orthodontists became interested in what we were doing. This culminated in a weekend retreat for the four brothers and four other "heavy hitters" in the orthodontic specialty facilitated by me and my dear friend and associate Alton Barbour. As a direct result of this weekend retreat my life and career experienced a major turning point. One of the orthodontists had recently been appointed as chairman of the orthodontic classes at the prestigious L. D. Pankey Institute for Advanced Dental Education in Miami, Florida. He asked me to assist him and teach management and communications at the Institute. Another orthodontist arranged for me to speak at the national meeting of the American Academy of Dental Practice Administration. Within six months I was so busy in dentistry I had little time left for other businesses. Since that time I estimate 90% of my professional activity has been in that profession.

"IF . . . "

- ✧ I hadn't been ill in the fifth grade and I had remained a good student.
- ✧ My parents had been more concerned about my schooling.
- ✧ Mr. Brenton hadn't challenged me with leadership.
- ✧ Jimmy hadn't talked me into joining the Marines.
- ✧ There hadn't been a huge spring snowstorm in Southwestern Colorado in 1952.
- ✧ Dynamite hadn't been handled carelessly.
- ✧ I had had one additional quarter of a dollar.
- ✧ I hadn't been introduced to the Dale Carnegie Human Relations Course.

During my life I have been in some happy places and some sad places, some difficult places and some easy ones. Some were painful and some were painless. Some were exciting and some were very dull. Some places were very safe and some were very dangerous. But never once, for one second, have I ever been in the wrong place.

Chapter Six

THINKING OUTSIDE THE BOX

T HERE ARE MANY FACTORS WITHIN US that influence
our decision-making. Some of them are beyond
our consciousness. The following letter from a dear
friend is a fitting and poignant lead-in to what is
unusual thinking in our society. If you have spiritual blinders I again encourage you to lay them
aside—at least temporarily.

Dear Bud,

I've just finished reading your book You are in
The Right Place, for the second time. I believe on
my first reading of it I was mostly caught up in
learning more about a dear friend, where he came
from, and how he thinks. That experience was
delightful. My second reading was just as enjoyable, and I found I was more in tune with your
message to the reader this time around.

I wanted to share a story with you, which
seems to fit your premise of student and teacher.
I call it, *The girl and the apple story.*

One day a little girl of seven or eight was
walking home from school. It was a day like any
other day. The girl was thinking about home,
what it would be like when she got there. Would

there be Mother or Father? Would they be drunk
and scary or sober and angry? Would there be
dinner tonight? Should she keep her dress clean
for tomorrow, in case there are no clothes ready?

While she walked and thought her usual
thoughts, she suddenly noticed an older lady
standing in front of her on the sidewalk smiling
at her, and holding out her hand with a gift of an
apple for the little girl. The lady said, "I knew it
was you coming; I could see your frown from a
block away!" She laughed and said, "Enjoy the
apple, and have a nicer day." Then she turned
and went back into her house. The little girl was
stunned. First of all, she seldom received gifts,
and fruit was a real treat, and this was certainly
unexpected. But more importantly, what did she
mean by frown? Something on her that shows
up a block away?

The little girl hurried home and pulled out the
old, tattered dictionary she had seen her big sister
use. She knew her phonics and could figure out
the spelling to find the word she was looking for
as soon as she got the page fr words. "To wrinkle
the brow. To, look with disapproval. To look down
on." Wow! She sure didn't want people to know
her THAT way from a block away! Right then she
sat down in front of the mirror and practiced facial
expressions she did like! First she just tried to get
rid of the wrinkles above her eyes. Then she started practicing to smile. She practiced every day.
Even though she was young, she noticed she felt
better when she smiled, even when she was just
learning. Every day the lady met her on the sidewalk with the gift of an apple. Finally she patted
the little girl on the back and said, "It is so good to

see your smile. I can see it from a block away!"
The little girl beamed, and continued to practice
that lesson for the rest of her life. She learned she
could feel better with a smile than a frown, even if
everything in her world wasn't wonderful. She
learned a smile makes others feel better too, and
makes them treat you differently. Through this
experience and subsequent "lessons," she learned
that we choose how we feel and act and those
choices help shape our moments, our days, and
our lives. She learned you never know when your
smile and outstretched hand or small token of car-
ing will make a difference in another life.

The little girl, Bud, if you haven't already
guessed, was me. I've never questioned that there
are teachers and lessons we learn every day. I've
always been acutely aware of my "teachers"
throughout my life: The role models I found in
women's biographies on the 3rd grade reading
shelf, the neighbors whose family life seemed
more like I'd like to have, the classroom teachers
from kindergarten through graduate school, my
own children, colleagues, patients, chance
acquaintances, Stan and you and Judy.

The big question to me is, why some people are
open to and ready to identify learning situations,
lessons and teachers, and others stumble along
missing all those beautiful opportunities to grow
and create what they want? I'm sure this question
is the crux of the issue John Bradshaw addresses
when he helps people realize that you can't save
your siblings from their dysfunctional pasts. You
can only save yourself. I accept this, finally, but I
still don't understand completely what is different.
Why can't they save themselves?

I believe every person, is confronted by teachers and opportunities to learn on a daily basis. For many, though, the apple remains just a gift of the moment, sweet, but over when the apple is gone. Inspirational stories remain a story, instead of a reason for hope and motivation. Good and successful people around them with happy lives and loving relationships are just seen as lucky, instead of role models to emulate.

I would love to see my question explored in your second book, Bud. At least, maybe you and I could give it a shot in discussion.

Thanks again for a thought provoking, warmly written book.

With Love and Friendship,

THE QUESTION:

"Why are some people open to and ready to identify learning situations, lessons and teachers, and others stumble along missing all those beautiful opportunities to grow and create what they want?"

For one thing we know that in all of the history of human kind there has never been an exact duplicate of you or me. Every human being is unique in the entire world. Probably the closest match in human beings is found in some identical twins. Many studies have been done that show similarities between twins, even when separated at birth. Yet they are different. There are countless family histories wherein one sibling became a highly respected citizen and the other became a hated and feared criminal. Why the different choices?

It is important for us to realize, as Elizabeth Kubler-Ross has told us, in-side every person there is a Mother Theresa and a Hitler. And it is God's promise that we are all given free will. We have a choice. We can choose to collaborate with our Mother Theresa (the God within each of us), or we can collaborate with our Hitler side, governed by our fear-based human ego.

Based on our responses to the myriad events and experiences in our lives a pattern develops. The pattern develops based on the thoughts we choose to entertain. We then seek to associate with others whose lives have a similar pattern. One of the early philosophers, probably Aristotle, said, "Birds of a feather flock together." A twenty-first century philosopher, Dr. Alton Barbour, a retired professor from Denver University, teaches, "Flocking together causes birds of a feather." This is further validation that our thinking which influences how and what we feel also directs what we do. Additionally this tells us that we are greatly influenced by the people with whom we associate.

A huge majority of Western society believes that each of us has one life to live. This is certainly congruent with the teachings of modern Christianity, and quite obviously would include all atheists. Reincarnation is likewise not commonly accepted among those of the Jewish faith except those who study and accept Jewish mysticism, the Kabala. In this "one life" belief system an immature person who makes poor choices that put him or her on a path of anti-social behavior is doomed to some form of perdition. I'm reminded here of an old Elvis Presley song, *In The Ghetto*. The ballad tells the story of a 16-year-old boy who grew up hungry and deprived of almost all of the amenities of life, including knowing his father. The song tells us that anger gets a grip on him and shortly he is "face down in the sand with a gun in his hand and his momma cries."

Is he condemned to hell or some other form of eternal punishment? Or, do we have a truly unconditionally loving, forgiving Creator with infinite patience, who only wants good for His/Her children but will not restrict their freedom? And does this Creator give us an infinite number of chances, through being reincarnated, to make choices that will bring us into harmony with the love of our Creator?

And then there is the matter of natural laws of balance. Is it as the Hindus teach, "Nature has a perfect accounting system ALL DEBTS MUST BE PAID"? Most Christians do not accept the Hindu teaching of karma. Yet, Jesus taught karma with two of his most widely accepted pronouncements, *"As you sow, so shall you reap"* and, *"Cast your bread on the water and it will be returned to you multiplied."*

If you sow hate, a derivative of fear, you reap hate. If you sow love you reap love. That's karma. If you cast disharmony on the water you will not receive peace in return. We can have it any way we want it! Isn't it wonderful to know we have such control over our own destiny?

Many historians have told us that reincarnation was part of the Christian teaching and was accepted by the Gnostics and by numerous church fathers, including Clement of Alexandria and Origen, both men of the 3rd century, and St. Jerome in the 5th century. The doctrine was outlawed and declared to be heresy in 553 AD by the Second Council of Constantinople. Disagreement over reincarnation between the Gnostics and early church leaders undoubtedly contributed to the annihilation of the Gnostics and the burning of the largest library in the world at the time, in Alexandria, Egypt. The library was the repository of nearly all of Gnostic scrolls.

It is probable that the Christian leaders thought the doctrine of reincarnation gave people too much freedom. They decided people should strive for immediate salvation. Many millions have not used their one lifetime to seek God but to seek the material and physical pleasures of this world. If the "one lifetime" doctrine is true we must surely agonize over the death of those who made poor choices.

I was first introduced to the concept of reincarnation as a young man in my late twenties. I read two books about the life of Edgar Cayce. Cayce was a psychic and medical intuitive who lived in Virginia Beach, Virginia. He proved on many witnessed occasions that he could accurately diagnose illness over long distance. [**Note:** A present day medical intuitive is Carolyn Myss whose work has been scientifically studied and whose results are widely known.] The Association for Research and Enlightenment has studied witnessed records of Cayce's readings, given while he was in a trance state, for more than 50 years.

My first reaction to the idea that we can live multiple lives reflected the fundamentalist Baptist teaching of my youth. I rejected it as the work of the devil. But by all accounts, Edgar Cayce was an honest and respected man, and very religious. My curiosity got the best of me and I picked up the book for the second time and read it through. The book was *Many Mansions* written by Gina Cermanera. I was then introduced to a second book about the life of Edgar Cayce titled, *There is a River,* by

Thomas Shugrue. After mentally digesting these two books my curiosity was insatiable. The more I read about the beliefs of other people, the more I wanted to know. My hunger to know has continued for well over 40 years. Being open to the possibility of reincarnation changed my life.

Dr. Brian Weiss, a Florida psychiatrist, has published two books in recent years describing actual case histories of patients that he treated by hypnotic regression. Hypnotic regression is often used to help troubled people recall mentally blocked-out events of their early lives as part of their therapy. His first book, *Many Lives, Many Masters,* clearly separated him from the mainstream of accepted thought in his medical specialty. His later book, *Only Love is Real,* gives case histories supporting reincarnation and soul mates from past lives.

During the years since being introduced to the theory of reincarnation seeking to gain spiritual understanding has dominated my reading and studying. I have read literally dozens of books, innumerable shorter articles, and listened to hundreds of hours of tapes and many lectures and conversations. Mental review, meditation, and focused thought has consumed uncounted hundreds of additional hours.

So what do I think I know as a student over 70 years of age who is seeking spiritual truth? Firstly, I must say, as much as I think I know, I have probably just scratched the surface. One of my frequent reminiscences is to marvel at how much more I know now than I knew one year ago. If it can be called a learning curve, mine is indeed a steep one. As I write this I eagerly anticipate the next discovery or awareness.

A few years ago I was speaking to an audience of about 200 people at a dental convention in Pittsburgh. My presentation was probably in the fourth hour of a six-hour lecture. A young woman in the audience raised her hand and asked, "Bud, do you believe in reincarnation?"

It was not an unusual question because several years earlier I had decided not to avoid spiritual topics if I thought they could be useful to my audience. In this presentation there had been numerous references to spiritual concepts such as: *Truth sets you free; As you sow, so shall you reap;* and *Cast your bread on the water.* In addition, I spoke of the benefits of avoiding judgments and being quick to forgive; and several references to the most important rule of all rules, the Golden Rule.

Two evenings before, as I was relaxing in my hotel room, that very question came to my consciousness and I thought through my answer, which I gave her:

"Yes, I believe in reincarnation, but it really doesn't matter.

What really matters is how we live our lives. In my case believing in reincarnation motivates me to have the objective of living by the highest standards I know."

Some of my beliefs about reincarnation have stood the test of many years of scrutiny, study, and thought. I shall be happy to help you understand my thoughts regarding this subject that I currently entertain.

Firstly and foremost, this belief does not impinge on what I accept as God's irrefutable promise—free will. There is a view, common among those who embrace the concept of reincarnation, that there are other spirit entities to help us with our decision-making after we have "crossed over." Yet, if I reincarnate it is my decision to do so. **The circumstances and events I will experience in another life are also totally my choice.**

So, why would I, or anyone, choose to reincarnate at a difficult period in history or into a dysfunctional family, perhaps with an inadequate body, or mind? Why would I choose a life of deprivation or pain? Why would I choose to be poor instead of rich, ugly instead of beautiful or handsome, gay or lesbian rather than heterosexual? Or to be a member of a persecuted minority race in the society in which I live? Most spiritual teachers who study reincarnation believe there is only one reason—the soul's overriding objective is to advance to an acceptance of our oneness with God.

As we know in our physical reality, in this life, our greatest opportunity for growth is when we are experiencing our greatest adversity. The same is true for the growth of the soul. If we have much to resolve, a long way to go on our journey home to God, we have the option of accepting greater challenges and maximizing our growth in this lifetime. Knowing I am one with God is the pure objective of the soul. In short, after deciding to reincarnate, with help from celestial guides, we design our own opportunities for balancing karma, learning lessons, and the opportunities for discovery and creativity.

A major part of my belief system is that we also have a cadre or band of spiritual entities—call them guardian angels or spirit guides—to help us during this physical incarnation. That belief extends to whatever we experience in our physical life and to the event of crossing over to the spiritual existence when we leave the physical body behind.

THE ANSWER:

So what is my answer to my dear friend who wrote the letter I used to introduce this essay? My beliefs tell me that she is an old soul who has lived many lifetimes. In terms of choosing how she will respond to circumstances and situations she chose for this incarnation, her decision to become loving and happy indicates a subliminal knowing that we create our own destiny in this life and whatever comes next. There is no question that we do not have answers for all of the vagueness and mysteries of life. Yes, faith is necessary. Accepting reincarnation requires faith. In part, faith that God has never, and will never, stop trying to lead us to truth and love and **never** gives up on **any** of Her/His children—even Hitler and Saddam Hussien. This belief absolutely allows me to take it on faith that there is no such thing as death. Therefore, there can be no untimely death either. Believing this makes life easier to bear, especially during times of adversity and turmoil. These beliefs are congruent with the knowing that God totally and unconditionally loves us *even when we make mistakes.*

In this incarnation for all of us there are many events that elicit questions. For some of our questions we find answers that satisfy our curiosity as it exists at that time. In my case there are a few answers I have discovered that have led to more questions. Yet other answers have led to opinions or beliefs, some of which have transitioned into "knowing" or "truths." Please keep in mind that my truths may not be your truths.

Some of the answers I have discovered (or perhaps been given), while I cannot in good conscience call them "knowings," have served to satisfy my quest for information and have allowed me to put a question aside or at least on a "back burner." For example: A burning question in my adolescent and young manhood years was, "Why is my brother Dan physically disabled and why I am physically advantaged?"

I accepted early on it was God's will, but I still wanted to know why. The theory of reincarnation has allowed me to put the question aside. To my satisfaction I have the answer.

Yes, indeed there are many events and situations giving rise to questions for which at our present level of knowledge and understanding we have no answers. Yet, I encourage every reader to give herself or himself the freedom to ask the questions.

We are taught that the answers to all questions exist inside us and that every problem contains the "seeds" that can grow into a solution. Our greatest limitation to tapping into this resource of infinite intelligence is fear—fear that it might not exist—or fear of what we might find if it does exist. We also must contend with another fear, doubting our ability to open and solve this mystery. Additionally there is the inability of the human brain to compute such theoretical ideas as; *Time is a human construct. Past, present and future are all one.*

One-half of the spice of my life is the mysteries. The other half is the chase, the excitement of the hunt and the courage to seek answers to those mysteries—fully accepting that in this lifetime I might not find all of those answers.

And let us not forget *Déjà vu* all over again!

TIME'S AWESOME FLIGHT

Today was just a speck of time
That flashed by in a whirl.
Yesterday was one of these,
Where is the Leader that guides my world?

The questions I ask, the answers are dim
I hurry when there is no need.
Please come back again O Time I have lost
And wasted without any heed.

There are moments I should just like to taste
That are part of memories dim light.
There are persons I should just like to touch
Who flew past me in times awesome flight.

But I still have tomorrow and some of today,
Opportunities won't end until I do.
I learn from my past and welcome tomorrow.
But not at the cost of now,
With you.

Chapter Seven

SPIRITUAL GUIDANCE

Extra Sensory Perception; Psychic Phenomenon; Metaphysics; Parapsychology; Clairvoyance; Clairaudience; Automatic Writing; Mental Telepathy; Telekinesis. For some people these words generate excitement and wonder—a desire to know. For some people they generate fear of the "Evil One" and for still others they generate scorn. This chapter also may encourage us to consider the existence of mystical supernatural Guides and Guardian angels.

The primary purpose of this chapter is to encourage readers to explore and develop their personal ability to dialogue with God.

M ANY PEOPLE BELIEVE THEY RECEIVE GUIDANCE from a spiritual source if they are receptive and listen. I am one of those people. In 1998 writer Neale Donald Walsch completed the final volume of a trilogy, three books titled *Conversations with God* with a subtitle *"an uncommon dialogue."* He has since concluded that it is not an uncommon thing—many people have such conversations.

I think meditation need be nothing more than just being quiet and receptive before, after, or even without prayer. But conversation requires two-way communication. I am completely satisfied I have received such communication many, many times in my life. I first experienced such contact more than thirty years ago as I was trying to work my way through an unhappy and unfulfilling marriage.

Many people refer to the process through which I received the communication as "automatic writing." At the time I needed help so badly I didn't care what anyone might have called it. Even though several spiritual people whom I greatly respected had described the phenomenon to me, and I knew the information was not coming from my own conscious mind, I was still very reluctant to discuss it. For several years I discussed it with no one except my closest confidants.

The circumstances during that period were the most difficult I had ever experienced. My marriage to my first wife certainly had its joyful moments, but as the years increased in number, whatever the bond was that held the relationship together began to fail. At a time when I was perhaps the most vulnerable to a tawdry affair I met the woman who has been my wife and life's partner for more than thirty years.

Prior to meeting her I never believed in any thing such as soul mates or love at first sight. My love for her only increased the agony of being married to a person whom I most certainly never wanted to hurt. In addition, we had two daughters, aged 15 and 12, whom I dearly loved. For about a year I lived what would best be described as a double life: Loving a divorced woman and her 7 and 3 year-old daughters while still living with my first family. At the end of that year I became seriously ill. My liver was functioning so poorly that the whites of my eyes turned dark yellow, as did my skin. I was hospitalized and examined by three specialists who were unable to agree on a diagnosis. On the evening of the third day in the hospital the doctors told me that if the bilirubin count in my blood did not improve in 24 hours they would recommend liver surgery. They informed me that my chances of surviving were about 50 percent. I was hurting so bad I told them I would accept the risk. Fortunately antibiotics turned the illness around.

During the illness I informed my wife of my infidelity. I also told her that if she were willing I would end my affair and make a diligent effort to rebuild our marriage. She agreed and I did make the effort, even though life seemed hollow and pointless. To my satisfaction I fulfilled my commitment to make a diligent effort.

An unplanned meeting with the strongest love of my life again turned my world into torment. It was at about this time that I became aware that I was incapable of solving my dilemma, and I began praying, meditating and experimenting with automatic writing on a daily basis. After prayer and meditation I wrote.

The automatic writing process, as I understood it, was to write words without thinking. I wrote on an ordinary tablet and when finished I put the writing in a convenient drawer. For the remainder of the evening I would watch television with my family, read, or putter around in my woodworking shop. A curious thing invariably happened—no matter how hard I tried I could never remember what I had written.

Later in the evening when my curiosity was insatiable, I would read the messages. The tenor of the writing was always loving. Over, and over the messages admonished me *to be kind, to be understanding, to be patient, to be gentle*. The messages helped but I didn't seem to be making any progress, and my agony went on daily. I was never free from pain and turmoil in my solar plexus and I couldn't remember my last good night's sleep.

One evening as I sat down to meditate, pray, and write, I again experienced the pain I had on my right side during the bout of liver trouble. I went immediately to a mirror and to my horror I could see a tinge of yellow in my eyes. I returned to pray utterly defeated.

All my life I had been taught that I didn't need help, that I could "kill my own snakes." For the first time in my life I realized I had a problem I could not solve. For the first time I said to God, "I surrender, I give up. I give my problem to you." That night I enjoyed a rare treat—a good night's sleep.

For the next couple of days I kept taking the problem back again. It was easy to know when I did, the pain returned to the pit of my stomach. It served as a reminder and I would say, "Excuse me God for taking my problem back. I give it back to you." Then I again would have a bit of peace.

A few evenings later as I read what I had written I was perplexed because the message was very different from those I was used to receiving. It was almost ominous. The message was: *"For the next few days your life will be like a sled going downhill without any rudder or any brake. Just hold on."*

I thought of the message frequently during the next day, which was quite normal. That evening a similar but more emphatic message came: *"You have a difficult time giving up control. We tell you, for the next few days you should surrender control and be like a grain of sand at the edge of an ocean, totally at the mercy of external forces."*

By now I was definitely intrigued, but I had no insight into what these messages meant. There was no instruction other than giving up control.

The morning after receiving the second message I experienced one of the strangest events of my life. I was driving to my office when without any preconceived plan to do so I drove into an apartment complex parking lot, walked into the office, and placed a deposit on a one-bedroom apartment. That evening after work I announced to my family that I would be moving out that weekend.

For the next several months my life was indeed like a sled out of control. Yet now there was a great difference. In spite of the turmoil, I experienced more peace than I had known for many years, and my life was trending upward. The divorce was final about six months after the separation.

I can pinpoint the exact moment my life changed. It was the moment I gave my problem to God. Over the next several years, from time to time, I again tried automatic writing. At those times I did not feel any special need to do so and the product was not significant. My spiritual studies continued to claim a large portion of my discretionary time, but two-way communications with God were not part of it until after my second reading of Neale Walsch's book, *Conversations with God,* Book 1.

I have never been the least bit confused about the value of the automatic writing during the most stressful period of my life. I have now come to realize that writing, as I concentrate on receiving messages from God, is still a very important activity, but not the only way to communicate. My handwritten journals have become the repository of hundreds of those conversations.

I have seen a bumper sticker that contains a somewhat humorous but very real message. It is: Why am I called devout when I talk to God but crazy when he talks to me?

Talking with God—Cases in Point

CASE NUMBER ONE

I was driving from Watertown, South Dakota due south to Sioux Falls in early May after spending two delightful days with a client friend and his family. As I was leaving the house just at daylight I was pleasantly surprised to find that my friend and his teenaged daughter had arisen early to give me one last hug before I left. As I drove south on the interstate I was on a spiritual high and as I looked to the east I saw a gorgeous sunrise. The uncommon beauty of that very common event elevated my mood to even greater heights.

After enjoying the sight for a few glances a low range of hills blocked the view of the sunrise. A mile or two later I again looked to the east and there it was to enjoy all over again—the red ball of morning sun creeping over the horizon. I thought, "How blessed I am to see two glorious sunrises on the same morning."

It was about then that I had an intriguing thought that kept coming back each time I rejected it. The thought was that I should enter into a partnership agreement with God. My internal argument against the thought was that whatever I would bring to the table would be so insignificant that it seemed audacious to even consider such a partnership. As I looked to the east again another low range of hills had again obscured the sun. Moments later I saw the third beautiful sunrise and to my great joy it happened **two more times!** All the while this thought about a partnership with God kept popping into my mind. My consulting experience has taught me that there needs to be some equality in what the two potential partners bring to the table. My contribution would be insignificant.

I finally said aloud, "God, how could that ever work?" The answering thought was clear and immediate, *"Bud, love bridges the gap."* That happened several years ago. The partnership is invaluable. I have since come to know that God wants the same arrangement with each of his children.

CASE NUMBER TWO

I had just completed a one-day personal and spiritual growth workshop based on the content of my first book; *You Are In The Right Place* for a group of about 30 men and women. A woman participant who knew that I had conducted a number of spiritual and personal growth retreats for men approached me to say that if I ever scheduled a series of retreats for just women she would definitely participate. I responded by telling her that if she could find about a half-dozen other women who would be interested we would schedule a series of four retreats. She was back within an hour with the names of the required number of participants.

After making the commitment I wondered what I had gotten myself into by agreeing to four, three-day sessions in an isolated, live-in retreat location where we would do all of our own cooking. Well before the first retreat was over I knew I would never hesitate to do it again.

The conversation with God I am disclosing here happened while I was driving down a two-lane mountain road in a beautiful snowstorm to return home after a three-day retreat with my women clients. While I was thoroughly enjoying the drive in my four-wheel drive truck I was wrestling with what seemed to me a contradiction in spiritual teaching.

From the time I was a small boy I have believed that God has intervened in my life from time to time. (Such as the series of quirky events that resulted in my being in the U. S. Marine Corps as reported in my book, *You Are In The Right Place.*) Yet in much of my spiritual study, especially *A Course in Miracles* and the *Conversations with God* books, God's irrefutable promise is that She gives us free will and She never impinges on it. I wasn't making any headway in rationalizing these two seemingly conflicting spiritual concepts.

On this beautiful morning, with dollar-sized snowflakes falling on my windshield, I once again spoke aloud to God: "Do you intervene in my life?" Immediately the question was answered with a question, *"Do you want me to?"* My answer was, "Yes." *"Then I do."* The perceived contradiction vanished like a snowflake on my warm windshield.

Talking With God

NOTE: The following "Talking with God" episodes have been selected from hundreds of conversations recorded in my journals over the past several years.

"High Best Friend."

Hi Bud.

"It occurs to me that today, just perhaps, my two friends and I experienced a spiritual breakthrough." [My friends and I realized during an informal spiritual retreat that we must also love and forgive our egos.]

You did.

"I knew you were present."

Bud, love is all there is to any success, even seeking enlightenment.

"Then why don't we have enlightenment now?"

I withhold nothing from my children when it is in their best interest. Today you heard of spontaneous enlightenment. That can be seriously misunderstood. Those who are said to have experienced it without diligently looking for it did in fact look diligently for it in past lives. It was in this life that it was most beneficial to all involved for it to happen. It does not happen without preparation and life experiences. Don't stop seeking.

✧ ✧ ✧

When you need me, you come to me. This is not a criticism.

"I've come to know you don't do that."

It is truly amazing how many people perceive me as "Judge." They would have me respond as one with an ego. I have no ego needs. I do not need your adoration or for you to worship me. It is serving yourself when you pray. Therefore I encourage it. As I told Neale Walsch, [Author of Conversations with God *books] it is important for your growth and well being for you to know me, trust me, love me, embrace me, use me, help me, and thank me.*

"How can I speed up the process to reach enlightenment? Would I benefit from a spiritual teacher or guru?"

Be receptive of guidance and counseling from any source that is founded in love. Remember, "When the student is ready the teacher will appear." This is not, just a Chinese proverb, it is spiritual law.

✧ ✧ ✧

"I'm glad I went to mass today with Dennis and Debbie. It is very obvious the service is greatly beneficial to many people. I hope I did not offend by not taking communion. My deciding thought was, 'First, do no harm.' I know that some Catholics would be offended by a non-Catholic taking communion. I'm just as sure it is immaterial to you. Am I right?"

Yes, but it is very important to your spiritual growth that you cast out every negative thought you have about the exclusionary nature of Christian churches. They are excluding all whom do not share their beliefs, but that exclusivity is important to them and if it hurts you in any way, join them.

"You continue to give me other ways to think about things. Thank you."

Your presentation on tolerance is a good one—not complete yet but doing no harm. Your growth will be better if you quickly cast out every negative and judgmental thought you have about dogma and ritual that is, or even may be, important to others. And get rid of that statement, "Ritual and dogma and doctrine are of men, only spirituality is of God." As you have come to know, I am, and have always been, in every person who helped evolve that dogma, doctrine, and ritual.

"Thanks, I needed that."

You are welcome and you are right.

✧ ✧ ✧

"Thank you for helping me learn to make the best decision for all concerned."

I am pleased that you have the presence to use spiritual guidance.

"You have also helped me know that I don't use you enough. Well, I'm working on it. I recall that I read in *Autobiography of a Yogi* that enlightenment is facilitated if the student is diligent with constant contact with the I AM presence. Seeking enlightenment is a major, perhaps overriding, desire for me at this time. I'm inclined to believe that if I am successful at improving my God consciousness I shall more nearly be able to achieve my other overriding desire to raise the consciousness of as many people as possible to accept four truths:

✧ We are all one.
✧ There is enough of everything.
✧ We need do nothing to earn your love.
✧ You are our best friend.

Another question—can I attain increasing levels of enlightenment, or is it all or nothing?

There are indeed degrees of God consciousness. That is what you see happening in the lives of many of your friends and in your own life. As you progress, the closer you get to full awakening, the more rapid is the process, until near the end there is a delightful explosion for some seekers. Others, because of their own obstinateness, block progress until it is like a dam bursting. It is important, if you are to love the entire journey, to remain unaddicted to your desired outcome. And remember my "time" is not your time—except occasionally when it is.

"Thanks, you sure are giving me good stuff."

❖ ❖ ❖

"Howdy, Partner, Best Friend,"

Howdy Bud.

"It seems I am being led into a deeper study of Eastern (Hindu) spirituality. Any comment?"

You are not being led. You are following the teaching of Deepak Chopra—the law of "least effort." You have come to your level of understanding from a healthy curiosity, which you have always had, without great energy-consuming effort. Remember, if it is difficult to grow you are on a lesser path. The path of love is never difficult unless your undisciplined thinking makes it so.

"Wow! Thanks. I see a 'new wrinkle' taking shape in the counseling of some of my clients. I have encouraged several to ask you questions and expect answers. It is amazing how many people are startled or even shocked at the recommendation."

Don't stop doing that.

❖ ❖ ❖

"I feel differently about praying to you in light of my recent acceptance—knowing—that you and I are one and that I co-create with you. Mind you, not as efficiently as I expect to in the future. But nonetheless very different than when I was not clear about our oneness!"

Of course it's different. It really started years ago when A Course in Miracles *told you, your will and mine are the same. It progressed from there through Walsch's* Conversations with God *books and really culminated with Deepak's book* How To Know God. *It will never be the same because you are starting to accept your responsibility for all outcomes. Therefore there is no going back. Do you want to?*

"No, but it was easier when you were responsible."

Sure, but was it as fulfilling?

"Oh, no. Yesterday I tried to identify my greatest fear. It is that I'm afraid of missing out—not taking full advantage of my 'new' relationship with you. It is almost a panic inside me."

Let it go. Remember the law of least effort and the law of attraction. If you are afraid, you are giving power where you don't want to! Think of what you desire and put all energy there.

"Wow. Thanks."

✧ ✧ ✧

NOTE: The following was recorded in my journal at 4:00 P.M. on September 11, 2001

"My question God, how will this beneficially contribute to your children in this world?"

I do not mean to be smug, but thousands of people are in a more peaceful place tonight than they were last night. Death is not to be hated or feared. Most of those who suffer pain and anguish or those who have lost loved ones, or those who survive with great physical and mental pain, you cannot convince that this is an opportunity to accept what is. The few who do this will experience the loss of the physical presence of loved ones but will know peace, as they never have before. It may seem unfortunate that most will live in fear, anger, hatred, and related emotions. It is their choice. But first they must accept that death, as you know it, is merely a transition for those that experienced it today. But here too, there is a choice. Be not dismayed. Stay the course of teaching love.

"Thank you. I shall."

✧ ✧ ✧

'It is pure joy to wake up each morning, no matter where I am and feel so blessed and loved.'

"Good morning God."

Good morning, Bud.

"Thank you for the privilege of being here and for enabling the above-quoted statement."

You are welcome, but you did it.

"I know that's true, but there is that strong motivation to thank you whenever I feel so great."

You can do much more co-creating with me. I will do little or nothing affecting you without your involvement.

"So many of my Christian brothers and sisters would have a terrible time accepting that statement."

Yes, and it is as you have written, they are in the right place.

❖ ❖ ❖

This entry is from late September 2001:
"This is a very tumultuous time in our world. I am pleased to see that I receive more mail advocating restraint, love, and prayer than I do mail advocating more violence. My heart and desire tell me that much good will come from this great violence for those that look for good. I most certainly do not choose for others to suffer that I might gain—anything. But it seems to me that if I govern my emotions and thinking with love it will be to my overall benefit, even if others choose violence.

Abandonment of ego is abandonment of evil. Evil begets evil. Stay the love course. My hand is open to you. The law, "As you sow, so shall you reap" is irrefutable.

❖ ❖ ❖

"Hi God."

Hi, Bud. Your ego is the reason you do not pick up the pen and talk to me. You might feel inadequate if great stuff doesn't get on the paper. Keep in

*mind, if you are out of your mind you are not in
charge of production. If you are in your mind it is
ego-based anyway. That doesn't mean that the
words won't be useful.*

"As I look back in previous journals, there truly is
some great stuff. I want more insights that can help
me stay focused and from time to time add a new
idea or concept or clarify a fuzzy area."

*Just as you tell your clients, "risk it." But in these
cases you have nothing to lose and the possibility of
much gain.*

✧ ✧ ✧

*In your attempt to make sense out of the disrup-
tion to your society do not lose sight of the spiritual
teaching "we are all one." Use every opportunity to
advance that truth.*

"Thank you. I will strive to do so."

*Another thing, reiterate in Changing Places the
conceptual truth we are, at any point in time, in
the right place—even those people who were in the
Pentagon and the Twin Towers on September 11. I
know many do not want to hear that and will angrily
reject you and your words. But the few who come to
that realization because of your willingness to be
rejected will reap commensurate benefits—ultimately
so will you.*

"Thanks."

✧ ✧ ✧

"Partner, the clarification and reinforcement is wonderful. The way of explaining cycles, everything returns to its beginning—wow! Cast your bread on 'the cycle.'

You have understood correctly. It has to do with everything—nothing is exempt. Realize also that at some times the circle is smaller than at others. Allowing for some returns to be short term and others to take a very long time. But the return of whatever you put on the wheel is inevitable.

"Karma, right?"

With an exception from your understanding of the eastern concept of karma—there is forgiveness of bad karma if the discovery is made from the mistake and if there is acceptance of responsibility.

"That's great information, and I think it should be in my next book."

Bud, there are no "shoulds," but it could be useful.

"Thanks again."

You are surely welcome.

✧ ✧ ✧

"You may be the only one I need to talk to today that I haven't. So here goes."

Shoot.

"I am indeed pleased with my increased ability to deal with unforeseen events such as the five-hour delay today while traveling to Hancock, Michigan. Also, at least at this point I am personally dealing with terrorist threats without fear.

On another positive front I am excited about the two presentations (tonight and tomorrow) at Finlandia University. My understanding on their expectation is that they want me to talk about the application of spiritual principles to life—personal and professional. That pleases me.

Also I am excited about adding a number of previous 'Talking With God' writings from my journals into *Changing Places*. It will be a 'piece of cake.'

It will also include ice cream for many who read the book.

✧ ✧ ✧

"Without question I can never say 'thank you' too many times."

Do you know why it is important? Well, let me remind you—I do not need recognition and reward. As you know I do not have an ego. The importance of saying, "Thank you God." is that it is your reminder that you are more fulfilled and happy when you are doing things that create the effect of your gratitude.

"Wow, thanks again."

And another thing about the recognition and reward you are receiving because of your recent offering of "Building Exemplary Practice." [a newsletter] It is recognition for your history of asking "How can I help?" even when you frequently thought instead "What's in it for me?" You have grown much, Bud Ham. Your future impact will be much greater than your past if you stay the love course and choose to learn.

"I hear you and I love you."

✧ ✧ ✧

How do you feel about putting spiritual growth on a back burner?

"Because of the recent understanding that you are not a jealous God and have no ego needs from me allows me to go with the flow. Certainly I'm not closing out spiritual growth and I am open to any intervention.

Good. You have heard and read many times there are no "oughts" or "shoulds" from me. Time is your friend.

"I'm curious and excited about what is next on my spiritual journey. I am truly receptive—maybe just resting."

It will happen all in good time.

"I must say it is so pleasant and comforting to know you don't need anything from me. But I need to give to you."

The time will come when you will not have that need. Look forward to it. OK?

"Ok. And thank you."

You are as always, most welcome.

✧ ✧ ✧

"Good morning God"

Hi Bud.

"The thought came to me, while I tossed and turned trying to get back to sleep, that maybe you wanted me to publish my conversations with you. This might communicate to people that anyone can have these conversations. I must be careful here because my ego might get involved."

I told you yesterday I would not let you write anything, said to come from God that would harm anyone. So trust that.

"It seems to me the nature and content of what I write needs to be a bit more of general interest and not so personal."

Why?

"Well who wants to read about my struggle?"

Millions!

"You probably know I have been looking for a publisher for *"You Are In The Right Place"* for a long time. Now I have started two additional books. Do you want me to publish my talks with you?"

You bet.

"Sometimes you sound a lot like me in your vernacular."

That shouldn't surprise you. I'm coming to the paper through you. And don't think you are the only one other than Neale Walsch. Can't you just imagine what would happen if everyone you know, who has read your last book started talking with me as you have? And thousand's—even millions more? When you started working on being your "highest and best," as instructed in CWG (Conversations with God) *book 1, you started spiritual growth at an accelerated rate. Everyone else can do the same. Your book will be at least an indication to others that Neale is not the only one chosen to help get the word out. You can bet there will also be others in addition to you. It is not a one person or few persons job—this saving the world!*

"Wow! That makes sense. But what if people just think I am an opportunist jumping on Neale Walsch's band wagon?"

Are you?

"Maybe."

So what? Will more people benefit and perhaps pick up their pencil and write down their highest and best thoughts? And wouldn't that move us experientially toward the kind of thinking that could make a great difference in a very short period of time. What if 100 additional authors successfully published their writings of conversations with me? I will tell you there will be more than 100! Do you want to be one?

"Absolutely."

✧ ✧ ✧

*Striving to accomplish your highest and best
versions of your greatest vision—your Grand Cosmic
Self—is prayer. Praise, to answer your question, is
achieved by recognizing my ability and desire to
help you. I don't need your praises—that would
indeed make me an ego being. I am not. Believe me
Bud, Love, Praise and Gratitude are for you, not me.
If you strive to continuously do those three things
that action will place you on the higher plane of
spiritual functioning, which does influence events in
your world. So stay in that mode as you do everything
from making phone calls, to writing, to shoveling
snow!*

"Thanks, that makes a lot of sense."

*You are on the path—just don't let fear and your
"pre-determined outcomes" distract you. I will help
you become!*

"Wow and thanks again."

✧ ✧ ✧

"I just realized at 8:45 that I had a 7:00 am breakfast
date with my friend. One of the things I have learned—
thanks to *ACIM* and *CWG* is that it's OK—I can apolo-
gize, which I did with a message on his answering service, and then release the fear-based feeling. You have
told me there is no chance or random-ness—but I still
hate to standup a friend or anyone!"

You released it, right?

"I guess I should say I'm releasing it!"

Yes, once you really let it go it's as if it didn't happen—you know that from A Course in Miracles.

"Yes, forgiveness is a great message. ACIM really helped me with that. It seems that perhaps the next step beyond—helping me know that what ever I do is your will for me—I pick it, accrue the consequences, good or bad, and hopefully grow closer to you in any and all events."

You've got it. But realize that that message will be very much misunderstood—it's as if I am encouraging "sin"—I'm not—just learning and spiritual growth—I shouldn't ever say "learning" because you already have all knowledge—you just don't know it.

"How can I tap into this information? Oh, I suppose I have on a few occasions. But I've read about it for 25 years or so—especially from Walter Russell's stuff. So can your instruct me?"

Sure. When you stay in your highest or best self—"Highest version of your greatest vision" you then feel deserving of great events—which include insights or information. Without this expectation nothing can happen. Your non-accepting, non-expecting attitude blocks any surfacing of the information, which is in your mind right now! So continue working on being what you seek to be—always, every second. It is no more complex than practicing the Golden Rule for others and yourself.
Love, Praise, Gratitude! Not just for me but for all of your brothers and sisters—at every opportunity!

And don't forget to apply LPG to yourself! Then the DOOR you've been reading about will be open any time you want to go "inside"—but you must expect the information or direction you seek.

"Thanks. I feel good about the answer."

❖ ❖ ❖

"Hi God."

Hi Bud.

"I still wonder sometimes if I'm really communicating with you. When your responses or messages seem forced I strongly suspect it is me—but wow, those times when I can't write fast enough and the times I receive information that was unknown to me, useful, exciting, etc. etc."

Of course the information comes through you—so your "screens" or "filters" affect the messages. But make no doubt about it I have given you more messages than you have written—more even than you could ever write.

"I'm concerned that recently my understanding of your messages seem to make it much less necessary for me to pray and meditate."

Bud, the key word is necessary. It isn't necessary. I don't withhold help from you, or guidance and intervention as you call it, whether you consciously try to communicate with me or not. But, you know how much better your thinking and being are in terms of serving your higher self when we have more one-to-one time. Communicating with me is like any thing else "you only get back as much as you put in."

✧ ✧ ✧

"Hi God."

Hi Bud.

"Sometimes I hesitate to sit with this writing pad and print the heading TWG. [Talking With God] I guess I'm afraid there won't be anything useful for me to say to you and I may not receive something that I trust is truly from you."

I understand the hesitation—but you have heard for years "he who hesitates is lost." Well, you won't be lost but that opportunity to talk to me will be lost and once gone it is irretrievable. My recommendation is always to plunge ahead when you have the feeling, the intuition. Don't think about it. In CWG I've said you must be "out of your mind." That just means don't think, just act. Thinking gives your ego, which you think is logical, an opportunity to let fear talk you out of writing. When you do what your heart tells you, you are out of your mind! A good place to be.

"Thanks. I thought that's what you meant but I wasn't sure."

✧ ✧ ✧

"Good morning God."

Good morning Bud.
Let me go first. Your concern about not spending enough time meditating, praying and talking to me is unwarranted. You have picked up a couple of key lessons from Conversations with God and are trying to implement them. I'm referring to staying more on track in your thinking about doing what serves your "highest and best," think more about total truthfulness, staying on task, etc. That activity is the real purpose of communing with me. It was great for you to go to mass with Tom and Carol. It is most important for you to honor the doctrine of any church you visit. In that church you were not invited to take communion. That is a ritual you do not need but it is very important to those that do.

"Yes, I now see it was arrogant of me to take communion in Catholic churches with the thought it was between you and me and to hell with their doctrines. I'll not violate that again."

That's just being tolerant!

"Thanks partner."

✧ ✧ ✧

"Hi God."

Hi Bud.

"It seems that I have a partial answer to my question. "Why do babies get sick?" Your answer, as I understand it is, "for a variety of reasons." You have also told me several times that nothing is left to chance—no accidents. That all seems OK to me, but if I had something more concrete it might clear up some doubt in other people's minds if I write about it?"

Would you accept that every baby had available to him or her detailed specifics of every illness he or she would experience?

"If you told me that was true I would believe it. But then the mystery of choice, learning, and praying comes in to fog up my mind. If it is all preordained why bother to pray for someone's health?"

Bud, pray for their peace not their health! You cannot know why anyone, baby or adult, is ill. And some things you don't understand must be accepted on faith. You are about out of time—let's return to this later.

"Good."

✧ ✧ ✧

"I can never thank you enough for the messages in the *Conversations with God* books. One I am really trying to put in practice is TELL THE TRUTH. It has become apparent to me how many times I have lied and not even felt bad about it. It seems others have been caught up in this sad state of affairs also. In one way or another, at some time or another probably almost all of my brothers and sisters, as do I, tell lies. I include in that observation that withholding information is also a lie. Thank you for helping me use this information to improve my life's activities and also to exert whatever influence I can to help people I work with do the same."

You have just assigned yourself another tall order.

"Yeah."

You can expect help from me but you must expect less than enthusiastic acceptance by most of your friends and clients and family members. Lying has been an ongoing blight on everyone's communication for each person's lifetime. Don't compromise your behavior but your course of action will require increased tolerance from you—more than you typically display. Remember your words, "I am not the world's policeman." Complete honesty, even when it's tempered by love can be a very scary thing for many

people. Proceed with your commitment. I will help,
but remember you will make a greater contribution
by being an excellent model than you will by being
an excellent confronter. I commend you for cleaning
up our own act. You have made a great start.

"Thanks. You're encouragement helps. But I must
say I am quite positive my effectiveness at influencing
others has shown marked improvements and that too,
is very motivating."

Your results will enhance the behavior of being
truthful with compassion and tempered by love and
tolerance, for those who are not ready yet to take
the giant step you have taken.

"This is part of the "tallest of the tall orders." This
honesty part can be part of every discussion and
statement. The opportunities to practice are almost
unlimited."

Keep the faith, Bud.

"Thanks, partner."

You are of course very welcome.

✧ ✧ ✧

PRIDE IS DARKNESS

Many things happen on the dark side of the moon,
They go untold because the stories are cold,
About men too proud.

All men stumble and many fall
On the dark side of their moon.
They cry alone because of pride like stone,
Won't use their friends.

God is all men and all men are God
On the friendly side of the moon.
They smile and laugh and are strong and gentle,
And use their friends.

Chapter Eight

PARTING SHOTS AT RANDOM TARGETS
THOUGHTS TO HELP US SLEEP BETTER

Great philosophy can be found in strange places. In author Tom Robbin's 1976, lusty, classic novel *Even Cowgirls Get the Blues* there is a philosophical gem that tells us mankind's problems are not political they are philosophical and until we solve our philosophical problems we cannot solve our political ones. Political problems cause humans to kill each other but the root causes of the problems are philosophical.

And so it is with us individually. One of the purposes of this book is to help readers clarify their personal beliefs and philosophies, and do so on a continuing basis, because as we grow they change.

Parts of Personal Philosophy

M Y PHILOSOPHY IS MINE ALONE, even though none, or at least very little of it is original. Dale Carnegie said he stole much of his philosophy from Jesus, Plato, and others. I shall be honored if you choose to steal some of my philosophy (mostly stolen from others) for yourself.

Dependence—Independence—Interdependence

Dependence creates fear and weakness. It creates weakness by causing a sense of inadequacy and leaves the dependent person questioning her ability to take care of herself. Additionally there can be the fear of what would happen if the one depended upon fails for some reason. When we are dependent our "God Part" is smothered and cannot grow.

Independence can create haughtiness, pride, and often intolerance of those less strong. It is a forerunner of despair and loneliness until we discover we were not created to stand alone outside of God. Our God Part is denied. In denial it is buried deep. Independence denies two great human needs—to give and to receive—neither is the greater. When we receive, we give to the giver the opportunity for him to give. It has been said, "Before one can be truly great one must be truly humble." Independence does not support any form of humbleness and our God Part can't grow.

Interdependence can start at a very early age. For example it might start with potty training a toddler. The baby learns a responsibility and the mother has given up some of her responsibility for the baby. The mother's smile and a kiss are the baby's rewards when he does well. He is pleased with himself. Love of self has started. He is still greatly dependent on his mother, but no longer totally so.

And so it is with us, the children of God. We cannot stand-alone and grow in this lifetime. God's work cannot be done on the physical plane without us. We depend on him and he depends on us.

Interdependence calls for giving and receiving. Remember, neither is the greater—our gifts to God, and/or his gifts to us. Love bridges the disparity and allows us to be happily humble, and our God Part soars.

Interdependence is God's plan.

FREE WILL

✧ God's promise is that She does not impinge on our free will in any way. Nor does She punish me for my decisions, some of which are mistakes. However my decisions have consequences, which I must bear. Not just penalizing consequences for poor decisions, but also positive consequences for good decisions.

TO BE HEALTHY

✧ Forgiveness is the single most important influence on our biology—our physical health. Without forgiveness our biography determines our biology. Our ego tells us we have a right to feel vengeful. Our heart tells us forgiveness is the best thing to do. If I choose to let my heart be submissive to my ego I will sicken my biology. [Thanks to Carolyn Myss for this insight.]

CAPITAL PUNISHMENT

✧ Peace cannot come to humankind as long we persist in taking God's power into our hands and kill those who kill.

✧ Humankind is not ready for peace as long as we deny life to another of God's children.

✧ The state that executes a human being is as guilty of murder as the murderer. We can tolerate it only because we widely distribute the guilt and it is easier to deny.

Our Experience Is Our Best Teacher

✧ It is easier and less personally threatening to listen to what others tell us to believe, based on their experiences and perceptions, rather than to accept the responsibility of interpreting our own experiences. It is wisely recommended that we not preclude discovery or learning from the experiences of others, but it is also well stated that our own experiences are our best teachers.

A Philosophy of Death

✧ An adequate philosophy of life must include a philosophy of death.

We are born unequal.
- Some are born into wealth some into poverty
- Some with beautiful, strong, healthy and functional bodies and minds, some with lesser

We live unequal.
- Some live many years, some only a short time
- Some accomplish much, some very little
- Some would describe themselves as happy, some as unhappy
- Some die easy without pain, some die hard with great pain

Death is the only equal event in life.
- Our physical body is left behind, pain filled or painless
- Even the wealthiest person leaves this life without a possession.

Some believe all of life is an accident—"chance" not "design." My thinking has led me to a different conclusion. There is order in all of nature. There is also purpose. We are well advised to ask, "What is my purpose?" We have been taught that there is a simple test to determine whether or not our purpose in life is finished—if we are here, it isn't.

We have a common purpose: *To become as much as we can with our uniqueness, our strengths and our deficiencies. To discover as many truths as we can from all available sources and the events in our lives and become as God would have us become. A secondary purpose is to help others become as much as they can.*

We are born unequal and we are unequal in our being. We do not have the same strengths and weaknesses, and we are not given the same learning experiences in life. We cannot know precisely what lessons we must learn in this life to grow closer to God or what pain we may experience. *"As you sow, so shall you reap"* confirms that there is no such thing as something for nothing, there is justice and being born unequal is part of that justice.

I do not believe in the concept of hell. Rather, I accept the first tenant of the Spiritualist Church, which reads: *The door to reformation and oneness with God is never closed to any human soul here or hereafter.*

When our mission is finished, whatever it is, there is no purpose to live longer in what we call life. There is no such thing as an untimely death.

Millie Mountain Rose

Today my Grandma died. Yes, I knew she would. She was 92. Her name was Millie. She had beautiful gray hair, lots of it. She was born in Indian Territory. Her mother was a Lakota, or Cherokee or Pawnee. We don't know, 'cause she wouldn't talk about it.

Her father, all 6 feet and 6 inches of him, a giant in his time, brought his half-breed children and his native wife to Colorado in a covered wagon when she was seven. They homesteaded west of Canon City. When she was eighteen she married and mostly tamed a wild stagecoach driver and cowboy racehorse rider. His name was Fred. He died ten years ago at 87. He was never sick. Maybe cigars, coffee, whiskey, bad horses, fat red meat and hard work killed him. She was much bigger than he and they loved each other.

Grandma used to raise turkeys. They were her
contribution on a ranch that was not quite large
enough. Grandpa always had a temporary job
somewhere usually doing very hard work. He
was 5'7" and he never weighed more than 145
pounds. That's probably too many. Grandma and
Grandpa never had a crossword or if they did no
one knew about it. They were almost always poor
by most standards. But they never fought. Maybe
they were rich and we just didn't know it.

When I was little, 9-10-11, I would stay with
them in their very un-ranch-house-like ranch
house. There were two large rooms. Grandma and
Grandpa had the large bed in the corner; I slept
with Uncle Truman and Freddie. Freddie, was my
uncle too, but younger. Aunt Barbara had a bunk.

In the early morning, when it was still, almost
cold, before sun-up, the grasshoppers were slow
and the turkeys could catch them easily. My
uncles and I herded turkeys until it got warm.
Their small yellow dog, Tawny, helped. We were
always starved by the time we returned to the
house for a huge breakfast. There would be big
stacks of sourdough pancakes, eggs, fresh side
meat (uncured bacon) and black coffee—if you
were more than 10.

Grandpa's momma was alive in the early
1940s—we called her Granny Rupp. She was
96 and had no teeth. She never reached 100.
We would see her on holidays—Uncle Buck,
Grandpa's younger and wilder brother would bring
her. Granny was less than 5 feet tall. Grandma
was very kind to her.

When I was 12 they moved into the big house.
A very ranch-house-like ranch house. The walls

were native sandstone quarried from down near the spring. Grandpa, Uncle Truman, Freddie and I loaded the stones. Rowdy and Joe pulled the wagon. They were matched grays and very strong. I got to drive them once when I was 11 to harrow a field. Grandpa said come to the house when I got finished. We did the field over, and over and over. When it got dark Grandpa came back. He had to help me turn loose of the reins. He was very proud. So was Grandma, but she never hugged me. It wasn't Indian.

Yep—she died today—I'm part Indian too. I didn't cry—yet.

Choices

My believing side says "Pain is inevitable. Suffering is a matter of choice. We create our own realities." My doubting side says, "There are few people who agree with that statement." My believing side says, "But that doesn't make it incorrect."

A person with a clarified philosophy of life is like a strong ship in a major storm under the guidance of a wise captain.

The anchor of a strong personal philosophy is faith—faith in one's self and faith in one's fellow man. But most of all, faith in the love of one's Creator who is love.

The greatest fear for many people is fear of the evil one, the devil. The greatest sham in the annals of fear in humankind's history is to blame any misdirected behavior on the devil. Yes, there is evil in the world but it is invariably caused by man. Until individuals stop blaming an external force—the devil—for their mean spirited conduct, he or she has placed a great retardant on his or her growth. To fear the devil is to fear ourselves and to believe God is impotent. Evil has no power man does not give it.

LOVE ENERGY

✧ Love energy is the source, the direction, the motivation and the fuel for every good work.

✧ Love energy multiplies the energy level of the one who selflessly gives love energy away.

✧ Love energy can be revived where it is dormant by forgiveness:

FORGIVENESS—THE *ESSENTIAL* FOR HAPPINESS

- Forgiving those who have hurt us.
- Replacing vengeance with forgiveness.
- Replacing fear and its derivative anger, with forgiveness.
- All things are lessons God would have me learn. If old pain from an event seems real be sure the lesson is not learned and un-forgiveness is lurking in the mind. When forgiveness is complete there is no old pain.
- Forgiveness has been accomplished when the negative energy responses such as: worry, greed, jealousy, anger, or revenge, are back filled by love and positive expectations.
- The highest quality of life is available to those who forgive others **and** themselves.

WHAT IS A CURSE?

✧ A curse is nothing more than a misused, misunder-stood blessing. Is it a curse or is it a blessing:

- To be born rich or to be born poor?
- To be intelligent or to be less intelligent?
- To be born of color or to be born white?
- To be beautiful/handsome or homely?
- To be physically disabled or to be physically advantaged?
- To be gay or to be heterosexual?
- To be born into this religion rather than that one?

THREE PARTS OF UNCONDITIONAL LOVE
Love—Freedom—Equality

Love without freedom is fear-based control.

Love without equality is conditional.

Only love with freedom and equality
can be unconditional.

A History of Marriage Ceremony

Marriage as a cultural institution and formality began about 2500 years ago, give or take few centuries, for most of the worlds' people. There is no question that it was designed as a hierarchical arrangement in almost every culture—husband superior and wife inferior.

The arrangement seemed to work satisfactorily for the cultural/religious societies of the past. But it is not working well today. The divorce rate has been around 50% for several decades and many of the remaining unions have little happiness. With the more liberal thinking of today the vows have been altered in many ceremonies. In recent decades the word obey has been deleted from the marriage vows of the woman in many Western society marriages. But the cultural behavior norms change much more slowly. What will serve humankind better?

Gifts and Commitments

I sincerely believe that one of God's greatest gifts to us is two edged sword, but one that is completely necessary for us to discover who we are and to learn and grow. That gift is free will—our creator never makes us do anything. (Would it make a difference if we reconsidered the Ten Commandments and accepted them as Ten Commitments?) Nor do I believe that God punishes us. The law of cause and effect and we ourselves take care of that very completely.

Isn't it interesting that we pay so little attention to the above mentioned freedom insofar as how we treat other people, especially those with whom we interact most? Would we have happier relationships if we didn't try to control others? What would happen if we gave up trying to control adults, including spouses, employees, co-workers, and even grown children? Wouldn't complete freedom contribute to their growth more effectively than our attempts to control them?

I'm reminded here of my hitch in the United State Marine Corps. As recruits we were told very early that those in charge could not make us do anything but they surely could make us wish we had done what we were told! As with every other life circumstance there was cause and effect. In this case very direct. I can readily under-stand why control needed to be so tight and swift in that situation. But in our day-to-day lives very little is so important that we should reduce another's freedom because of our control needs.

I like Deepak Chopra's statement in his book *Seven Spiritual Rules for Success*. "The Universe has a perfect accounting system—all debts must be paid."

Most Christians tend to shy away from the Sanskrit word karma. But Jesus taught karma when he said, *"As you sow, so shall you reap"* and *"Cast your bread on the water."*

In my work, I am pleased to serve as consultant, counselor, advisor, teacher, and mentor. Sometimes I wear all five hats in the same intervention. Because of the nature of what I do, sooner or later I become involved in some form of family or relationship counseling with about half of my clients. I don't mind at all, it just goes with the territory. One of my clients and his spouse asked me to suggest a few guidelines that they could use to help them in their relationship. I was happy to oblige. They are as follows:

Commitments for A Happy Marriage

FREEDOM

God gave us freedom, which is the greatest gift I can give my spouse.

✧ I shall strive to increase my spouse's freedom, which enhances our love, peace and harmony. This includes the freedom for each of us to pursue interests we do not share.

✧ I commit not to misuse freedom or violate a promise, which would also be destructive to our love, peace and harmony.

EQUALITY

God gave us different talents and the opportunity to learn from each other.

✧ I shall accept our differences with tolerance and gratitude.

JUDGMENT AND CRITICISM

Any attempt to judge another person exceeds my capability. Constructive criticism is an oxymoron.

✧ I shall work diligently to eliminate these two destructive behaviors in our relationship.

OPENNESS AND HONESTY

Truth with compassion never encumbers us. The perfect blending of trust with love is wisdom. Truth sets us free.
✧ If my spouse does anything that offends me I shall tell him or her, "That doesn't work for me."

DEFENSELESSNESS

Defenselessness is love-based offense.
✧ When my spouse yields to temptation and judges or criticizes me I shall not defend. Defenselessness is strong not weak. My defending would compound the negative energy already present.
✧ If I make a mistake, I shall admit it.

DECISION MAKING

If I make more love-based decisions, I live with more love and less fear in my life and I am therefore happier.
✧ I shall strive to make all decisions from a love-base rather than a fear-base.
✧ I shall consider my spouse's reaction to a decision prior to making it.

INTEGRITY

Responsible reliability is an essential ingredient of a healthy marriage.
✧ Say what you will do and do what you said you would. If you change your mind, tell your spouse.

FORGIVENESS

The most perfect spouse will make mistakes.
✧ I forgive myself, my spouse, and others so I may

be whole and healthy. If I am whole and healthy my marriage can be whole, healthy and happy.

✧ ✧ ✧

If Given a Choice Would You Choose Happiness?

Duh! Is that a stupid question or what? Of course you would choose happiness, right? It would seem to be a no-brainer, yet I ask you to carefully consider the following components of the antithesis of happiness:

- Have you forgiven the person or company that never paid you—for whatever reason?
- Have you forgiven yourself for a bad decision that appeared to hurt others or yourself?
- Do you still experience hurt, anger, sadness, etc., when remembering an unexpected turning point in your life that thwarted your desired outcome?
- Do you still experience old pain when remembering a criticism or other unkind words that caused you pain in the past?

If you answered "yes" to any of the above questions you have chosen to be a victim rather than choosing happiness. Victim hood is the antithesis of happiness. You cannot be a victim and be happy at the same time.

The following simple, self-administered exercise is guaranteed to raise your happiness level if you *choose* to spend the few minutes working through it— remember life **is** choices!

To "Raise the Bar" of My Happiness

Make a list of the events in your life, that when recalled, cause you to experience old pain.

✧ If you are willing to look hard enough *and honestly want to see it,* you will see the Silver Lining of that dark cloud and the perfection of that event.

Make a second list of the names of every person (including yourself) who has wounded your spirit— "hurt your feelings."
✧ Use whatever process is acceptable to you to forgive each person. You will know when you have been successful when you think of the old incident and there is no old pain!

Remember, pain is always pain of the past. The past does not exist except in our mind.

Overcoming Fear, the Second Killer of Happiness

Worry is fear of the future. Just as with pain of the non-existent past, fear is always fear of the future. Since the future also is non-existent we do not have to defeat fear, just ***release it.*** The following process can teach you how to do it.

What we know about worry:
✧ It ranks among the highest of the controllable factors causing human suffering, misery, depression, suicide, and illness.
✧ It is more common than the common cold, and for those who suffer from worrying it happens more frequently. However, unlike the common cold there is a cure.
✧ Worry is a choice. Millions of ordinary people have been successful in training themselves not to worry. Henceforth they live with greater happiness.
✧ Worry runs in families, but it is not hereditary.

Worrying families have a worry teacher in each generation. It is most appropriate to love him or her, but it is totally unnecessary to continue to carry the burden they gave you.

✧ Worrying about a fear that does not exist gives the fear validity in our mind. Worrying also saps our strength, and reduces our ability to cope with the future, if the worry becomes our reality.

Does this mean we never take precaution or make preparations? Of course not. If the national weather service issues a flood, or hurricane warning it is prudent to take precautionary measures such as moving to higher ground or boarding up our windows. Prudence and caution are not fear unless you allow them to become fear.

Please consider the following:
- "Spirituality demands prudence."
- "Faith cancels fear."
- "We become what we think."
- "Whatever we focus our thoughts on becomes greater."
- The truth is that we are responsible for what we think, because it is only at this level that we can exercise choice. What we do is a direct result of what we think.
- If we think fearful thoughts we become a frightened person.
- When you are fearful you have made a wrong choice.

Giving Up Worry by Using a Worry Log

The main requirement for becoming worry free is to realize that the freedom which comes from being worry free is a desirable state. Said another way you must want to give up worry! If you have been taught that to be a responsible adult you have a duty to worry, you must first undo that teaching.

- Who was your worry teacher?
- How old were you when you were taught to worry?
- As a mature adult must you still accept that teaching?
- Are you willing to try to become worry free?
- Are you willing to accept the Holy Spirit's teaching, "All is well, have no fear, I am with you?"

If you are now ready to give up worry it is a simple process that only requires a bit of personal discipline and a few minutes every time worry reduces your effectiveness.

The Worry Log

Steps to overcoming worry:

1. On a clean sheet of paper write "Worry Log" and today's date.
2. Make an itemized list of everything you are worried about right now.
3. Considering each item separately ask yourself, "Other than pray, can I do anything about this?"
4. If the answer is "No" draw a heavy black line through the item and say, "I will pray about it but I will not waste my energy by worrying about something I cannot change."
5. If the answer is "Yes" then ask, "When?" If the answer is "now" **just do it.**
6. If the answer is, "Yes, but not until Monday when I am back at work," make yourself a note and commit to taking care of it on Monday. Draw a

heavy black line through the item and say, "I refuse to waste my weekend worrying about something I cannot take care of until Monday."

Frequency of Use

Create a new worry log any and every time you have that nauseous feeling in the pit of you stomach. My experience in working through the process, carefully and thoroughly, is that frequently within thirty minutes the solar plexus pain—the "gut ache" is gone. When you finally experience this you will know you are making progress. But even if you do not experience this after many sessions of completing the process do not give up. Remember, you have been a worrier for many years! If you periodically review your Worry Logs you will prove to yourself the futility of worry!

The other killer of happiness is fear—fear is always fear of the future. It doesn't exist either—except in our minds

Giving Up Anger through Forgiveness— A Personal Experience

One evening as I returned from a consulting trip my youngest daughter asked me to visit with her for a few minutes. She told me she was pregnant and was dropping out of her senior year in high school to marry the baby's father.

I did not handle the announcement with maturity, love, and kindness. Later, after studying *A Course in Miracles* for about a year, I came to the realization that my anger was having a painfully negative effect on the lives of our entire family, and especially on the relationship of my daughter and me. *The Course*

teaches that forgiveness is the path toward oneness
with all people, which is a requirement to oneness
with God.

I called her into my study one day after praying
and meditating about my problem. I told her that the
needed love-based action was forgiveness, and that I
had become aware of the penalties for continuing to
live with debilitating anger. I forgave her and I asked
for her forgiveness. Our relationship was healed
immediately. And now, years later, I can tell the world
it was a permanent healing. Not so incidentally, my
grandson is one of the brightest lights in my life.

✧ ✧ ✧

Learning Principles which have and are Influencing
My Thinking and Therefore the Quality of My Life.

✧ Curiosity is a gift. It is never inappropriate to ask
questions—sometimes silently, sometimes aloud.
✧ The natural tendency in humans is to trust. If we
are non-trusting it is a result of choices we have
made in reaction to some of life's more painful learning experiences.
✧ We do not, at the conscious level, choose all of
life's learning episodes. We have the ability to choose
how we will respond or react—and therefore control
what/or if we will learn (or otherwise benefit) from
the experience.
✧ It is appropriate, useful, and congruent with spiritual teachings to have visions, goals and objectives. It
is inappropriate, detrimental and incongruent with
spiritual teaching to be attached or addicted to our
predetermined outcomes. Have visions, goals and
objectives, but go with the flow, accept what happens, and keep your head up.

✧ Truth sets you free. This is one of the greatest of the simple spiritual truths.
✧ Love is the most powerful force in our existence. The way to keep it is to give it away. No one ever has too much love. We can multiply how much love we have by freely giving it away without aforethought or selection.
✧ Love is the most practical, readily available tool we have. To teach love overtly or covertly may well be humankind's highest calling.

✧ ✧ ✧

Discipline and Responsibility

One's quality of life increases dramatically when one develops the discipline to be responsible for his or her *thoughts, words and actions.*

THOUGHTS

If we choose not to entertain the mean spirited thoughts that come to us we can prove to ourselves that we have the power to control our thoughts. It is imperative to accept that we become what we think which places us in control of our own destiny.
✧ If we think love-based thoughts we become loving.
✧ If we think fear-based thoughts we become frightened.
✧ If we think mean-spirited thoughts we become angry and offensive.

The law of attraction states: *We attract to ourselves things and events that we fear and hate or things and events that we love and cherish.* The factor determining the nature of what we attract is our thoughts. Thoughts have powerful but unseen energy and are the "money of the mind." It is "thought currency" that "buys" (attracts) that on which we focus our attention.

The required first step for a person to create the future they desire is to take full responsibility for their thoughts. Every creation of humankind began as a thought. This is true whether noble or ignoble— whether a material thing such as a garden rake, an airplane, a computer, or an action such as murdering someone, or creating the Salvation Army, or choosing to love someone.

WORDS

To attempt to live a life of love we must be ever mindful and selective of the words we say. Once said, a word is irretrievable—we cannot take it back no matter how much we might like to. Poorly chosen words can wound, maim, or kill. Properly selected words can heal and add to life's fulfillment and joy.

ACTIONS

"By their actions you shall know them." We become what we think. Our thoughts lead to our words, be they beautiful or base. Our actions are the manifestations of our control over our being. We must be ever mindful that our actions begin with our thoughts, over which we can achieve positive control.

PARTING SHOTS AT RANDOM TARGETS

Poetry to Help You Sleep Better
(by the author unless otherwise noted)

POETRY CAN ONLY BE A GIFT TO ANOTHER POET. So who is a poet? One who writes poetry? Yes, but aside from writing, a poet is anyone who sees beauty in the world and helps others to see that beauty and their own beauty and completeness.

QUESTIONS

If I loved you once
Do I love you now?
Could it possibly not be?

Have you forgotten the ecstasy?
Did you think it was all just hormones,
The body's desire to reproduce itself?

Have you forgotten the longing when we were forced
apart?
Does your heart quicken still, decades later, when
you remember our first kiss?

Wasn't it beautiful to see only perfection in your
hearts desire?
Isn't that really what God created?

Did you think you were naïve not to see flaws?
Can we have it the way we want it and still call it
truth?

Must we accept the imperfect seen in the world's
eyes?
Can we choose to see only the perfect from God's
eyes?
Isn't perfection, as beauty, in the eyes of the behold-
er?

Do I love you now?
Yes!

ODE TO MY BUDDY

Note: By Brad De Coux, Toledo Bend, Louisiana.
In memory of his friend, Gregory P. Massey.

Rest assured, God is caressing, His exemplary little boy,
Who deeply loved his family, and played with simple toys,
Tracked fins and feathers, friends and foes, as an honorable man,
To adjudicate heartfelt justice, then hunt and fish for joy.

Though many times departures, appear untimely and much too quick,
It seems, in fact, that is how the Lord's best examples are picked,
While far too many of the rest of us, in this ego driven land,
Require a lot more lessons, even hard-toed armored kicks.

The boy can now be with us all, each minute of every day,
He has no schedule conflicts; he knows every fact and way,
We all should seek his counsel, while bearing that in mind,
In times of sadness yet to come, and future do and say.

Reasons for life are now cloudy, though clearly they are not gone,
For Love, Compassion and Honesty are solid, not gilded stone.
Eventually, with the passage, of extremely testy time,
Certainly, the basis of this tearfully written rhyme,
We once again will genuinely smile, we may even truly laugh,
And at that point, Greg's comfort, will clutter up the graph.

FRIEND

I call you friend, for that portrays my feeling.
And it, upon reflection, is a word appealing.

Friend, we've shared our joys and in our troubles
tried.
We laughed when we rejoiced and suffered when we
cried.

I call you friend, for this depicts so true,
What I would like to be, if I could be like you.

TEARS ARE RAIN

There are days when sadness wells up in our eyes
And it's very hard to believe
Tears like rain that falls from the skies
Can help us to perceive.

The beauty around us that was hidden by pain
Though in truth for a little while
We sank in our sorrow and it seemed like an age
And we failed to see the smile.

That came from God as a ray of sunshine
Or from the heart of friend
Tears wash out the dust of the past
And show us a clear tomorrow

Goodbye sorrow.

ODE TO A COWBIRD

Do you know the lowly cowbird
Is hated by those who don't know
That she can't change her habit
Of never sitting a nest,
Nor hatching her chicks,
Nor being there to see them grow.

She lays her eggs in a robin's nest
Or a lark's or a blackbird's home.
Should she be condemned
For fulfilling nature's plan
Or praised for doing her best?

There is a lesson here for us my friend,
For those that are haughty and proud
Who look "down their nose" at another man
Because of his station in life.
If he does his job
And gives it his best
Should we ignore his strife?

I've heard it said and you have too
That all men are created equal.
If that is so and in God's plan
The greatest of us is the same.

BEACH STORM

It rages now, this storm I'm in
And I am miles from home.
The lightning flashes and thunder roars
And it thrills me to the bone.

The waves are crashing on the beach
As a giant symphony,
With regular beat and blended tones
Of wind swishing through the trees.

I know I am part of God's own plan
As I am standing here,
And blessed with opportunity
To feel nature without fear.

Sea birds are flying valiantly
Above the crested waves.
They are headed home where that may be,
Should we think they are brave?

I think not, it seems to me
They are doing what they must.
Responding to the storm naturally
With Mother Nature they can trust.

And now I'm back inside my door
But I can still look out,
And hear muted sounds on shore.
Dear God help me know what life's about.

INVICTUS II

(With reverence and respect to John Henley
who wrote INVICTUS in 1863)

*It is my choice to keep or give
My counsel and my struggle.
To arch my back and stiffen my lip
And remain in charge of this, my trip*

*I knew my struggle to become
Put the wind in my face.
None but I could change my pace,
Or accept release with grace.*

*I am the master of my fate.
I am the captain of my soul.
None but I can choose to give
To God or not, this life I live.*

ON BEING ALONE

When did you last fly away
On wings no one could see?
Where did you go on that long trip,
And why didn't you go with me?

I've tried so hard to find my way
And never share my pain.
I have not known the loving part
That others seem to gain.

Is it a choice to go alone
And hold to the narrow path?
Or take a place that I can share
And soar with another half?

It has been said we all need friends,
No one is an island.
Let us take the dare and travel there
And share a future planned.

But you should know that there must be
A time I stand alone.
To fill my cup and drink it down
Knowing I am not wrong,
Or alone.

CHANGING PLACES

and going

TO ANOTHER RIGHT PLACE

is always a choice

T H E   E N D

M Y FONDEST WISH FOR YOU, as a reader of this book, is to develop your own list of beliefs and "knowings" that will become your personal guiding philosophy. In this regard I encourage you to question beliefs, values, and your current knowledge or knowing. Benefiting from this examination is greatly facilitated by faith in the guidance of a higher power because growth requires change and change is not without risk. There is a strong argument that tells us that the greatest risk is not to take risks. Personal growth is spiritual growth and is more likely to occur when the seeker has an open and inquiring mind and is willing to risk.

I am pleased and grateful for the opportunity to share my personal philosophy, poetry and experiences in this book. If it is appropriate for you to use any of my guiding principles, values, beliefs, philosophy or knowings, please be my guest. Yet, I strongly encourage you to use the information in this book *and information from any other sources* merely as springboards, a starting place, for the development of your own guideposts on your path of spiritual growth.

It is critically important for us to **own** our values beliefs, knowings, and philosophy. We cannot own this life guiding information unless we are willing to thoroughly and openly examine each component, and sometimes even to test it. We must accept that growth requires a willingness to change our guideposts. To accept life guiding information totally on the authority of anyone else is to imply that you are governing your life by a set of imposed guideposts which, without examination, you cannot own. We are much less likely to violate any components of our life guiding system if we own them, thereby avoiding the guilt and frustration that can be the result of attempting to guide our lives by someone else's system to which we are not fully committed.

Seekers of truth are not always right, but they are always learning and growing. Be a seeker!

www.ingramcontent.com/pod-product-compliance
Lightning Source LLC
Chambersburg PA
CBHW071530040426
42452CB00008B/963